EVERYMANIA

EVERYMANIA

The History of
THE EVERYMAN THEATRE
Hampstead
1920–1926

by its founder
NORMAN MacDERMOTT

LONDON
THE SOCIETY FOR THEATRE RESEARCH
1975

First published 1975
by The Society for Theatre Research,
14 Woronzow Road, London, N.W.8

ISBN 0 85430 024 4

Published with the support of
The Scottish Arts Council
and the Harold Adler Memorial Trust

Printed and bound in Great Britain by
Morrison & Gibb Ltd., London and Edinburgh

CONTENTS

ILLUSTRATIONS

Foreword

Towards the end of 1972 the Society had the surprise pleasure of making contact again, after a long silence in his Scottish retreat, with one of its founder members and benefactors, Norman MacDermott. He told of a manuscript he had completed on the history of the Everyman Theatre which he had founded and managed in Hampstead in the 1920's, and for which he was seeking a publisher.

The Society had an interest immediate and practical; here was a first-hand account of a significant theatrical venture from a period half-century away and too sparsely documented. The interest for my part was more personal and nostalgic; here, in the reference to *Through the Crack*, the Everyman Christmas production in 1920, was the forgotten source of the earliest of my own well-remembered theatrical experiences.

The manuscript was a lengthy one, discursive and with many an aside. In offering to prepare it for the press it was necessary to abridge certain of the reminiscences, but at all times the intention has been to refrain from changing the original style and, as I hope, to keep the flavour of the author's own personality. It is the author himself telling, in his own words, the story of his ambition, his aims and achievements.

The story is a remarkable one. The impact and influence of the Everyman in the years between the wars has proved greater and longer-lasting than its own short career. An enterprise of innovation in its day, it has set a pattern for many later developments and practices now accepted as custom. The theatre structure itself, revolutionary at the time with its single-rake floor and absence of footlights, finds itself the progenitor of the Mermaid's improvisations and the design of other purpose-built theatres. Its front-of-house policies regarding cast lists in alphabetical order, latecomers, and bookable seats at all prices are still only now being adopted by progressive managements. Its experimental policy, then in isolation, has been taken up by many other similar small fringe theatres in outer London and the provinces. The establishment of a resident company, the attempt at true repertory, and the encouragement to new writers has found a parallel in the efforts of, for instance, the Royal Court in our own times. *The Vortex* has a claim to be regarded as the *Look Back in Anger* of the inter-war years.

A theatre which, Ellen Terry apart, attracted the talents of Edith Evans, Athene Seyler, Felix Aylmer, Leslie Banks, Raymond Massey, Claude Rains, to single out but a few of many eminent names; which gave first-nights to plays by Drinkwater, Chesterton, O'Neill and Coward; which brought the canon of Shaw into popularity with a new generation—and all this at a time when subsidy from public funds was unknown—deserves the recognition which it is now earning in the legend of stage history. The fact that it found a use for the Poel curtains and the Craig screens is symbolic of the role it played, as a link, in keeping the traditions of true theatre alive at a time when standards in most other places were moribund.

In its achievements the Everyman was unique, and its 'begetter', Norman MacDermott, has himself shown unusual prescience in the way he has meticulously preserved its records over the years. Now that this material has served his purpose in the writing of this history, he has generously given his archives, through the Society for Theatre Research, to the British Theatre Museum where, in its new home in Somerset House, they will be available for more detailed research by other historians. This is an example which might, with credit and advantage, be followed by other managements and individuals engaged in the theatre.

The Society, and the Author, wish to acknowledge the generous financial support received from the Harold Adler Memorial Trust and the Scottish Arts Council towards the cost of the publication; to the Society of Authors on behalf of the Bernard Shaw Estate for permission to print the extract from the talk which forms the Introduction to the book; those many friends who have helped with advice and to solve points of detail in the narrative; and Jenner Martin and Madelaine Wolfe who undertook, voluntarily, the typing of the original and final text.

Finally the Society would wish to thank the Author for giving it the opportunity of including his book in the series of its annual publications.

JACK READING
Editor for
The Society for Theatre Research

November, 1974

An Introduction

by

GEORGE BERNARD SHAW

THE PRESENT PREDICAMENT OF THE THEATRE

being a verbatim extract from a talk given by him
at the Hampstead Town Hall on

Thursday, 15th May, 1919

(Mr. Norman MacDermott in the Chair)

I am not really going to give you my views on the present
predicament of the theatre. It is not a matter of view, but of fact,
and for me personally, an extremely hard fact; and I want to-night
to describe it to you. I am not an amateur of the theatre and
therefore cannot gush about it. My point is that if you are going
to have a theatre of an artistic nature you will have, for some
time to come, to provide it for yourself. That is not a consequence
of the theatre becoming less popular, but more so. You must
remember that in our time a curious thing has been happening.
Owing to the generalisation of education, the knowledge of
reading and writing, which have been spread by the Education
Act of 1907, you have what I call a double action. You have a
real spread of artistic culture going on at a low level, but the
consequence is that art, such as there was, of a higher level has
got starved. . . .

I suppose those of you who contemplate the theatre as it exists
in London to-day will admit that from a commercial aspect the
prospect is extremely rosy. There are more people going than ever
before, enormous sums are being made, and I presume being lost;
but when you turn to the artistic aspect it is desolating. You
cannot see a play of mine anywhere. You have not had the
opportunity for a long time past and will not have the pleasure for
some time to come. I do not say that managers of theatres are so

sagacious as to perceive that it is no good producing my plays. They occasionally appeal to me to put on my plays but I have to explain to them that they will ruin themselves, and, although they are sure they wont, I have to save them from themselves and they dislike me very much in consequence: the authors who ruin them are much more popular with them!

In order to lead up to an explanation and to gratify my taste for economics, which is keener than that for the theatre, I will talk of the economics of the theatre. You will probably imagine you are interested because it is about the theatre, and I shall be interested because it is about economics.

Let us begin with the economics of art. If you compare the business of introducing art to the public you will find that there is one quite extraordinary difference between the artistic attraction and the general article of utility. For instance, you want to buy bread—and now that the rationing has been removed you do it very easily—but when you have consumed the loaf then it is done for and gone. The baker has to produce another loaf before he can serve another customer. With a work of art this does not happen. If it is a picture, you can go and look at it until you are tired, until nothing would induce you to look at it again, but the picture is as attractive as ever. You may go to one of my plays until you have had enough—say 30 times—but when you have got to such a pitch that you would go to see anything in the world rather than that play again, the play is still as good as ever, and probably attracting other people. So that, you see, in a work of art you have a sort of philosopher's stone: something that does not waste by the consumption and therefore this exhaustion commercially is never produced by the work of art itself. What is exhausted, of course, is the appetite of the consumer for it. . . .

When you get a continually successful play as a play, you will find people go again and again. That was very important to me when my plays were being performed at the Court Theatre under the management of Messrs. Vedrenne and Barker. I do not know how often people went, but there is no harm now in letting you know that I never spoke of the audience, but of the congregation, because apparently they came always like going to church. Instead of every Sunday they came every day. That is perhaps a slight exaggeration. It is sometimes rather trying for an author if he happens to be there, as he sometimes is, when he knows his best joke in the play is coming and he hears people turn round and tell others it is coming, and in the wrong way, and generally spoiling it. But anyhow that involves the fact that they must have seen the play several times, and that was what occurred in the Court Theatre. . . .

There is another point. If you take pictures, churches and theatres, they are rigid structures—no one yet has invented collapsible ones—you cannot, as in many commercial instances, adapt the fluctuations of supply and demand on the part of the public. You have to average your expectations of the business, and you must build your theatre of a certain size. In addressing any gentlemen of business who are here—and whom I want to interest because they have money—I want to point out that they must be very careful how they judge the theatrical business. They will probably feel if they are asked to contribute to an artistic theatre that they want to know if it will be managed in a business-like way. It does not matter in the slightest degree.

And this is the reason why it does not matter what you pay in a theatre. If you go to one of these Napoleonic American men—for instance, my friend Charles Frohman—the man who was believed to own thousands of theatres, but as a matter of fact only owned one—he was a man who understood theatrical business. What was the attitude of that man with regard to paying the staff, even to paying authors? His attitude was this: Bring me a success and I do not care what I pay. Bring me a failure and I will cut it at the earliest opportunity. He was perfectly right in that respect. . . .

Now I come to the question to which all this is preliminary, and that is: When you build a theatre on what calculation do you build? You must have in your mind some relation between the cost of erecting the theatre, the prices of admission, the number of people it will hold, etc., because your object in building a theatre is not to serve theatrical art, but solely for the purpose of making money. When you have built it you do not go into it but get rent from it. That immediately puts a limit to the amount you spend on actually constructing the theatre. . . .

I come nearer to the existing situation. Before the war, roughly speaking, the estimation on which you built a theatre, the size you made it and the rent you got from it, was this: that if the theatre—taking the average of successes and failures—was three-quarters full on Saturday night and half full on all the other

3

nights, the management could scrape along and pay the rent. It is true that it could not be made to pay without hard work on the part of the management and occasionally it was necessary for some benefactor to come to the rescue. The Court Theatre, for example, was one which for some years managed to produce plays of a high class, and it paid its way. I may tell you as a private matter that when the Vedrenne-Barker enterprise was started at the Court it had no capital. It began with *Candida*. In order to make that possible a few people, one of whom was my wife behind my back, guaranteed £200. My wife guaranteed £50 and a few more the rest. That was all that was necessary. As a matter of fact it was not necessary to call in the money. It gradually grew from giving Matinées to giving performances at night. So the Vedrenne-Barker campaign went on and for four years did good work. It involved hard work and also a course of conduct wildly uncommercial. You had to have a management which had the nerve to go in for popular stuff in which there could be no failures. To say a play should be performed for two or three weeks, whether the house was empty or full, and to withdraw it at the end of its time even if very successful, was a very hard thing to do. . . .

I have come to the end of the economics. I now come to the war. . . .The playgoers of London practically disappeared during the war and you had this audience of khaki men. Whereas before the war you had a rather *blasé* audience, you had an audience now for whom you could not get anything old, silly or childish enough. At the Alhambra you had Mr. George Robey racking his brains to think of the simple crudities for which before the war he would have been thrown out of the house, but he went on doing these old things amidst roars of laughter. . . .

The theatres were jammed full—it was no longer a question of being half full. So that if a theatre was let to someone who would produce a play with twin beds, etc. it would be at an increased rent and the estimation would be based on the house being full every night. Now do you understand why theatre rents went up beyond all reason and the continuance of Mr. Granville Barker's campaign was made impossible? Rents have now gone up on the expectation that theatres will be full every night and that is the reason why the higher drama has disappeared from the theatres, unless there is a generous supporter at the back of them.

It is time I should stop. I will very soon, but I want to see if I have forgotten anything. . . . For many years I have been associated with several ladies and gentlemen who have been trying to establish a National Theatre. At the time of the Tercentenary of Shakespeare we proposed having a theatre to be called the Shakespeare Memorial Theatre with an endowment of half a million. We had a committee and we did a great deal. . . . We spent a lot of money which we threw away. We got one subscription of £70,000—that was magnificent. There were some Englishmen who came forward, but I am sorry to have to tell you that the man who put down the £70,000 was a German. That is the estimation in which the theatre is held in this country. There is clearly no use in going to work without an endowment.

The artistic theatre has been driven out of the West End. There is only one place to go, and that is to the suburbs. There you have low rents. Expenses have gone up so much now that it costs more to run the cheapest theatre in London than it used to cost to run the St. James's; nevertheless you fortunately have Mr. Arnold Bennett and Mr. Nigel Playfair to control the Lyric Theatre at Hammersmith and they have got hold of *Abraham Lincoln* by John Drinkwater which has been a great success. He would like to put that piece on in the West End, but he cannot get a theatre because they are let at these high rents. London cannot live by Hammersmith alone. Here in this district you have a large congregation for a great theatre. It is proposed that this theatre shall be put up in Golders Green. I sincerely hope it will. If you want anything like an artistic entertainment in the theatre you must have a suburban theatre of your own, you must have something not subject to West-End rents and under entirely artistic management. Mr. MacDermott has a project of that kind. The whole business of my coming here to-night has been to get you into the room in order that you may listen to him. You will now have an opportunity.

"I don't know what comes over you all up here. . . .
It's a mania . . . a MANIA! . . ."

EDITH EVANS

Overtures and Beginnings

Before the first world war my interest in the theatre had been in gathering articles and illustrations about the new form of the German theatres and the new scenic ideas from abroad, knowledge of which was then only just filtering through to the British stage and its public. I was planning a lecture for the Liverpool Playgoers Society on *A History of Stage Decoration* from the earliest Greek times to the present day and had been collecting, or having made, about two hundred lantern slides to accompany it. I had also been designing and making models of simplified settings for Shakespeare, Ibsen and others, and these had been shown in the foyer of the Liverpool Repertory Theatre where they were seen by the Irish Players on their way to a season at the Royal Court Theatre in London. A new production of Synge's *Deirdre of the Sorrows* was being planned and W. B. Yeats asked me to make a model for it. Shortly a telegram asked me to take this and other models to London to be seen by Lady Gregory, and I duly displayed them in the large top room at the Royal Court which is now itself a theatre. Afterwards we went back to the auditorium where I sat at the back while my work was discussed by a group of three or four. I was asked for an estimate of cost. A rather more intense discussion followed and then Yeats came to me and said, very gently, "I am so sorry, but the old lady says NO". This phrase became famous: I do not know that this was the first time it was used but it shattered all my surging hopes and I returned disconsolate to Liverpool.

Not being in Health Category A, I was in a 'reserved occupation' in the head office of an insurance company in Liverpool but, leading a protest over aircraft insurance, had resigned. This led to arrest as a conscientious objector and a period when, technically 'on the run', I re-conditioned a cottage for my mother in the Welsh hills. My pre-war interest in the theatre had been revived by an article in *The Nation* in January, 1918, "Wanted, an after-war

7

Theatre" by the editor, H. W. Massingham, in which he wrote: "What a contrast! For the outer world, the most frightful reality; the last word of human surrender and reckless devotion; in the mimic world of the theatre the mincing of the dilettante and the coquette." This was followed by two important articles over the signature of an initial 'B', which in turn were followed by a joint letter from three conscientious objectors in prison. These were Hermon Ould (later Secretary of International P.E.N.), Horace Shipp and Harold Scott, the actor and later a permanent member of the Everyman Company. Then came a letter from Miles Malleson full of interesting information about the American 'Little Theatre Movement'.

This American 'Little Theatre Movement' was initiated in their universities, some of which had established drama courses and had built theatres on the models of the ancient Greeks or of the German Littman form. Unhampered by war restrictions the movement had spread rapidly and other experimental theatres had been opened such as the Greenwich Village in New York, the Provincetown Players (Eugene O'Neill's starting place) and, ultimately, the fully-professional Theatre Guild of New York. Through the *Christian Science Monitor* I had made contacts, and received books, magazines and leaflets. Some of their leading scenic artists had been in London on their way to Paris and had called on me. From these sources much valuable knowledge of the French, German and Russian theatre came my way.

After April 1918 until the Armistice there was only sporadic airing of theatre reform in the press or in periodicals but much interchange of proposals in private correspondence. I wanted to follow up *The Nation* lead by action. Someone, it was felt, must be in London co-ordinating ideas and efforts and to provide a meeting point for those interested, otherwise the impetus that had been roused might just relapse. Unfortunately the most alert of the correspondents were in uniform or in prison, and it was put to me, as the most active of those free, that I ought to undertake this task.

It happened that a colleague of my wife (who was not fully in accord with my anti-war stance) offered us the tenancy of her small Chelsea flat for the duration. So it was that, in the summer of 1918, I arrived in London with my wife, her Singer sewing machine, a quantity of Spanish wine-jars salvaged from a wreck

8

Illus. 1 & 2
Scale model for the six-hundred-seat theatre proposed to be built at Hampstead
Garden Suburb or at Golders Green. Exterior and interior. This project was
never realised but the feature of the steeply raked auditorium floor was incorporated in the conversion of the drill hall which became the Everyman Theatre

Model made by the author

Illus. 3 & 4
The Drill Hall at Hampstead
Above as a Whist Club on the day of take-over
Below, four months later, after conversion as the theatre

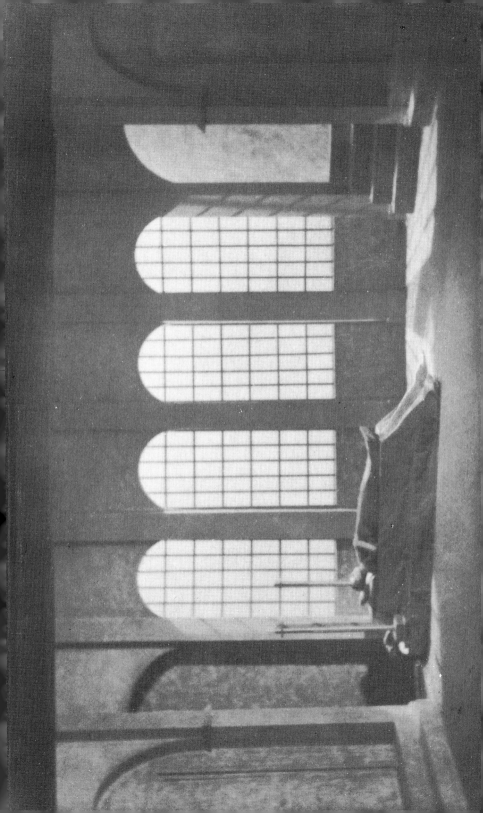

in the Mersey and, in my pocket, my total worldly wealth of twenty-seven pounds. I did not know one person in the whole of London. Of immediate importance was to make a living, and the Spanish wine-jars were a vital factor. These I enamelled in simple patterns in bright clean colour and took them to Heal's. I made jewellery in copper, silver, and sometimes gold, some of which was bought by Liberty's and the rest by a folk-art shop off Theobald's Road run by two dear ladies who also found work for me decorating flats. I found a wood-turner who made from my patterns copies of Chinese-shape vases which, enamelled and fitted as electric table lamps, had a steady sale at Peter Jones in Sloane Square.

I took part in the Shakespeare Birthday Celebration at Stratford, helping Miss Edith Craig (Ellen Terry's daughter and Gordon Craig's sister) to set up an exhibition of theatre material, scripts, costumes, scene-designs and models, including my own. I was asked to give three lectures there for a Summer School. The scene-models later went to Amsterdam for the British Section of the International Exhibition which was shown afterwards at the Victoria and Albert Museum.

Miss Elsie Fogerty asked me to take a class at the Albert Hall for her Central School of Speech-Training and Dramatic Art and every Friday afternoon I instructed eight or nine charming young ladies. They were among the year's debutantes and were at the school really to learn deportment and similar graces. What they thought of the class is not recorded but they learned the correct way to hold a saw: I was paid three guineas for each lesson and that was life-saving manna.

I took the Aeolian Hall and gave my scenic-history lecture. During the lecture I ventured to say that while Gordon Craig was an inspiration to designers he was not a practical man of the theatre and, showing a slide of one of his most famous drawings, I pointed out that the proscenium arch for it would require a steel girder over sixty feet long, an engineering feat not then possible. At the end I was approached by a delegation of Rutherston, Wilkinson and Lovat-Fraser, designers for Barker in 1911, and was told that if I continued to denigrate Craig I could not expect their support for my theatre scheme. I never saw any of them at the Everyman! I also started an illustrated magazine, *Theatrecraft*, on the model of the American *Theatre Arts* magazine,

back page: Illus. 5 Romeo and Juliet. Juliet entombed.
    Muriel Pratt as Juliet. 1920 (See page 24)
opposite: Illus. 6 Arms and the Man. Raina's bedroom. 1922
    (See page 44)   Author's photographs

which I handed over to Hermon Ould and Horace Shipp from the third number to free myself for other theatrical undertakings.

I had telephoned to Miles Malleson, referring to his *Nation* letter, explained who I was and a meeting was arranged. We had lengthy talks of schemes and plans until we reached agreement on a first stage for practising our ideas. It seemed clear to us that, if support were to be gained on an adequate scale, some example of new-style production must be shown, no matter how modestly at the start. Accordingly we planned a mobile unit that could be transported at short notice to any hall in or around London with a programme of one-act plays of which there was a great store unaccepted by conventional managers. We had no doubt there were eager audiences waiting for such entertainment. We realised also that, for the impact we wished to make, no amateur production would suffice; the acting and production must be of top standard and the staging and lighting must show forth the new principles. The first programme would consist of Drinkwater's $X=O$ in which, set on the battlements of Troy, three young warriors of another age discuss war. With this would be given one or more short plays of Lord Dunsany, of Malleson's own, and of others.

We rented a disused store in Bloomsbury for twenty-five shillings a week, brought in one like-minded acquaintance who was a skilled cabinet-maker, and at weekends and in evenings we constructed a set of four pillars two-feet square. In the hollows of each were retractable curtain-runners on which curtains hung, creaseless, immediately ready to surround a stage, and a blue sky-cloth. We made also some collapsible platforms and steps to give varied heights. A few floodlamps and spotlights with some dimmers completed the equipment. Malleson gathered a small group of actors of like thinking, bored with the West-End theatres. He produced the plays, I fixed staging and lighting, and the cabinet-maker took charge of the whole setting, transport and erection.

Throughout these activities I had met an increasing number of people to whom I could talk of a new theatre project. Malleson had taken me to meet Gilbert Cannan, translator of Rolland's *Jean Cristophe*, and also the author of *The Joy of the Theatre*, a small book but radiant with enthusiasm. Introductions spread to influential people and I became convinced there was enough eager support to make such a project practicable. Particularly strong interest was shown by residents of Hampstead Garden Suburb led by Mrs. S. A. Barnett, widow of Canon Barnett one of the Garden Suburb Founders. Because of the analogy with the *Everyman's Library* I made myself known to its editor, Ernest Rhys, and he took me to see old Mr. E. J. Dent. Both gave their names as Councillors and Mr. Dent was one of the first substantial donors to the Working Fund when it was opened. It was now that I made the acquaintance of Bernard Shaw and made my first visit to his Adelphi flat. He gave me much good advice, recommending me to take up gambling on horses instead of trying to reform the British theatre; but he did agree to speak at a Public Meeting. This was held in the Hampstead Town Hall on the 15th May, 1919, before a packed audience.* William Archer and St. John Ervine also spoke in favour and I outlined my own proposals. There was no doubt about the eager welcome for the scheme.

A short time before I had taken a modest one-room office in Great Russell Street opposite the British Museum and here was displayed my scale-model for the projected theatre (*Illus.* 1 & 2). I had leaflets describing the scheme printed and was sending them to everyone I thought would be interested and to names given to me by new supporters. Interested by the publicity, people began to call for more information. One of these was Lord Dunsany who became a Councillor and donor to the Fund. The press showed interest and descriptive articles appeared in the *Westminster Gazette* (a strong supporter), *Manchester Guardian*, *Daily Telegraph* and others including the literary weeklies, *The Nation*, *New Statesman*, Orage's *New Age*, Lady Rhondda's *Time and Tide*. *The Studio* had an article with coloured plates of my scene-models and *The Architects Journal* printed an article on the theatre-model with photographs. The Pelican Press took great interest in our printing and new type-faces, such as Garamond, used with sepia ink on a parchment type paper, were adopted for all our publicity work.

Strong pressure now developed for the theatre to be built in Hampstead Garden Suburb and a site was offered on the main square opposite the Church. It was thought by those who had inspired the Suburb that its ideals would be properly realised by

* Extracts from his speech form the Introduction to this book.

the grouping of Church, Community-Centre and Theatre as its hub. I believed that the theatre should be a theatre for London and not for any one small enclave having to rely for audience on a limited number of residents, especially as the Garden Suburb was one of the most inaccessible spots in the metropolis. After long discussion a compromise was reached. Under the aegis of the Suburb Trust the theatre would be built at Golders Green where the Hippodrome already drew large audiences from surrounding districts served by buses from the station yard. Directly opposite the covered station approach was a vacant plot of land of good size and on this an option was secured. Preliminary plans were prepared and submitted to the London County Council but consent was refused. A new rule governing new theatres was in force which stipulated that they must be on an island site. Our plans would have provided for the building to have passage-way on three sides but the fourth would have abutted on the back of a row of shops. The search for a home started afresh. I consulted Bernard Shaw, Galsworthy, and others. They were all strongly of the opinion that the theatre should be in Hampstead which, with its leaven of authors, painters, actors, lawyers and other professionals and progressives would, they thought, provide the regular nucleus of an audience for the theatre we contemplated.

Finally, in the spring of 1920, I found what was to be our home in the heart of Hampstead. Near where Holly Bush Vale and Heath Street converge at the Hampstead Tube Station I came upon an old Volunteer Drill Hall. It was repellent: bare brick, Victorian varnished wall-lining, bare iron girders. It was being run as a rather shady *Palais de Whist* on which the police had turned a jaundiced eye (*Illus.* 3). To escape further vigilance, the leaseholders, who had grown nervous, were glad to transfer the remaining years of their lease for a nominal premium. At last we had the shell of our home.

The Prologue

Swords into Ploughshare

This title is apt, symbolically, because in driving a new furrow for the art of theatre we were obliged to convert war material into a ploughshare. The restoration of national industries necessarily took precedence in the demand for all materials. In the building trade where stocks of bricks, timber, plumbing and electrical goods were practically non-existent, rigid control was imposed on the limited amounts of new material that were available. A non-profit-making venture in the Arts stood very low in the scale of priorities. We were given a permit for only £1,000, a quarter of our application. This alone would have meant the postponement, if not the abandonment, of the proposal to erect a new building and even, if we were to secure a home for our work at all, in the plans for the conversion at Hampstead many of our ideals had to be sacrificed. Some, however, I was determined to keep, such as a steeply-raked auditorium floor, the level stage, and lighting without footlights.

These were months of intense and exciting activity. Detailed measured plans had to be prepared, then submitted to the London County Council, to Hampstead Borough and other Authorities for approval, perhaps modified, but certainly argued about fiercely. In their way, our plans were revolutionary: the steep rake of the floor, no fire-curtain, dressing-rooms under the auditorium, the use of soft-woods (no hard-wood being obtainable) and a score of structural details. No architect was employed, nor any building firm contracted. The whole of the work was carried out, except for a little brick-work, by direct-labour craftsmen recruits who later jelled into the stage-crew. Many of these stayed on throughout the story until my last day in the theatre.

We were harassed by Inspectors. They came from the L.C.C. Architects Department, the District Surveyor Office, the Fire Brigade, the Sanitary Offices, and, of course, they depended on their Books of Rules while we needed to get round or under them. Some of these officials officially objected but became generally helpful: others remained obstinate and obstructive. A floor-rake at the angle we proposed had never existed in a London theatre; a fire-curtain between stage and auditorium was a *sine qua non*; dressing-rooms under the auditorium were anathema in spite of the steel and concrete floor between: artistes would smoke and set the whole place afire, choosing a time when the theatre was full to capacity so that audience and house attendants would be fried. Stage-lighting fittings sited in the auditorium were even worse: they would explode and terrify the audience who would panic and jam all exits, leaving the artistes to be stifled in their inferno below.

The struggle was prolonged but I was very determined and eventually won a hearing by the L.C.C. Theatres Control Committee. At County Hall I was shown into an impressively large room with a big horse-shoe table behind which sat some seven stern-looking gentlemen. They were very courteous and listened to me patiently while I pointed out that in New York, where fire regulations were notably stricter than in London, no theatre with under five hundred seats was required to have a fire-curtain; that in the new type of theatre widespread in Germany the floor-rake might be twice as steep as we proposed; that the staircase hazard in many London theatres was infinitely greater than could exist at Hampstead where there would be only 300 seats and three exits with direct access to the street; that the building was completely detached from any other and stood on an island-site. I was asked a few questions while they conferred in low voices. Then I was told they were interested in the information I had given which would be studied and that I would be advised later of the result formally. I rose to leave and as I reached the door I was astonished to hear the Chairman, Colonel Levita, call: "The best of luck to your venture". Shortly afterwards we heard that our plans were accepted, subject to inspection during the work, and that the building would be licensed as a temporary measure renewable by annual application; and so it continued until it became a cinema.

Then commenced a hurried search for building material that could be bought cheaply as war-disposal or as scrap. The country was littered with Army and Air Force temporary structures, some unused, some not even completed. Wooden hangars for small planes were dispersed on farm fields and one of these in Buckinghamshire was our first purchase. Dismantled and transported to London it became the disputed raked-floor of the auditorium and also the flat stage. Our next purchase was an unfinished Army latrine and ablutions hut of timber framing covered with asbestos sheets. This became the fireproof proscenium-arch, the dressing-room partitions, and sundry fire-break doors. The end window of the building on the street side was taken out and the brickwork cut away to form a lofty scenery-door. Another window on the same side was similarly altered to provide an extra exit, direct to the street, level with the front row of stalls. It was our intention to brick-up the remainder of the eight large windows in both side walls to shut out weather and light, but we were told they must remain as additional exits in case of fire. The Inspector's imagination did not follow ours in picturing bejewelled ladies being hoisted by noble males up to the window-sills where they would come face-to-face with rugged firemen, axes in hand, smashing the glass to let them scramble through. . . . I quoted the fire-fighter's first rule—CLOSE all doors and windows to prevent draught—but he remained obdurate. To block out the daylight these windows had to be covered with heavy curtains. By the good offices of Ambrose Heal I met Sixsmith who manufactured fabrics for export to African territories where rolls of them would, along with cows, become the dowry price for wives. I went up to Lancashire to his factory where I was shown, in storage sheds, ten feet high pyramids of large balls of the rough cotton dyed in colours so bright that they seemed to glisten; an unforgettable feast for the eye after the grim grey dirtiness of war. I chose an orange with broad black stripes running the length of the weave and was allowed to buy rolls of the woven fabric at a cost rate that made them practically a gift. From this were made not only the black-out curtains for the auditorium to which it gave a welcoming gay effect, but for other windows throughout the building, and for doors to artistes' dressing-rooms.

We knew that the most likely building snag would be the rake-angle of the auditorium floor, but by now had learned caution and not to face Inspectors with shocks too abruptly. Over a weekend therefore the stout under-framing to carry the floor was rushed up: this openwork did not look so very steep and was allowed to stand unclad until after the next inspection. Then on another weekend the floor-boarding went down. Compared to the usual stalls floor it seemed like an Everest, but once down who would order it to be torn up? Fortunately it was another and more reasonable Inspector who came next.

The seating was of two kinds. The side-blocks were rush-bottom church chairs supplied, again through Mr. Heal, very cheaply. The centre seating was of the tip-up type with padded arm-rests, bought second-hand from one of the closed cinemas and re-upholstered. When the 230 were delivered, in separate parts, they were piled in mounds of iron frames, seats, arms, backs, with sacks of wedges to counteract the floor-slope. Then one warm August night a very tall man and a small youth arrived and set to work: the youth set-up the iron standards and the man followed with an outsize pump-screwdriver and his apron pocket full of large screws. Stooping over he pumped four screws into each standard and the seats were slotted into place. He never un-stooped, but like a machine worked along the rows. Neither man nor boy spoke a word until about one o'clock they asked whether they could have a cup of tea? Then they resumed the standard-screws-pump routine monotonously. Some hours later the backs and arms were quickly added and by five o'clock in the morning I found them tidying-up and packing their kit ready to catch the first city-ward tube train (*Illus.* 4).

The proscenium opening was closed by a set of grey velour curtains that neutralised the eye for whatever they would disclose. These, with the window-curtains and the fibre floor carpet, had all to be heavily fire-proofed. It took a week for the carpet to dry out. It had been intended to hide the girdered roof with a false ceiling which would also have the effect of keeping the auditorium warm in winter and cool in summer. But that would have had to be a builder's job and costly. Expenditure by this time was patently over the £1,000 permit and checking officials had begun to ask questions. I argued that as most of the material was bought as war-disposal, or second-hand from junk yards, it did not have to be included in totals as the permit was for new material. Some-what grudgingly this contention was accepted. But many gallons of paint would be required to cover the oppressive varnished timber that was everywhere including the roof-lining. Five gallon drums began to arrive of the aluminium 'dope' that had been used for painting the anti-Zeppelin balloons which once had glistened in the sky around London. This was used to paint the roof-lining and girders.

On the side of the cul-de-sac opposite to the new scenery-door was a disused Fire Station with large quick-opening doors for the engines. A lease of this also was obtained and the ground floor engine room became our scenery workshop. Though on the small side, it was more than valuable: flats or built-pieces could be run from the workshop straight over the street on to the stage, or could be struck and rushed across to the workshop to prevent cluttering stage-space. In plays of many scenes, when construction had been delayed, pieces were sometimes painted in the street during an act, much to the amusement of interval-strollers. When run onto the stage they would change colour under the heat of the lamps but we had learned the tricks of distemper, even though the smell of the size would permeate the house.

Some time previously the carpenters had started to divide the basement into dressing-rooms with partitions and doors made from the fire-proof asbestos sheeting. One day the negating Inspector arrived and said, "No doors". Also that the partitions must stop short of the ceiling by one foot. We pointed out that the ceiling was of reinforced concrete on steel beams: we pleaded the decencies. But argument was useless; he did not bother to give any reasons, merely reiterated "No doors". Curtains of the African material were duly hung. From his obduracy, however, one good thing resulted. There could be no back-biting nor slander back-stage at the Everyman, for every word spoken could be heard. To the end of the Dressing-Room section and the Green-Room with its full height 'last-look' mirrors, a double-sided fire-proof door of the asbestos on timber frame was placed. Mr. 'Negative' condemned this and insisted on an iron self-closing door in an iron frame. This was duly ordered and the frame placed in position for cementing. At this point another Inspector came and condemned the iron door as too heavy for its position, and required a teak frame with a teak door. By this time, exasperated beyond limit, I had the original asbestos door replaced and stained brown. It was still there five years later.

Alterations were made to the original entrance-way to form a small foyer. Here exhibitions of paintings, drawings, posters and of imported continental wares such as Bohemian glass, Viennese silks and table-ware were to be shown. A Box Office was in one corner and in another corner a small Bar for dispensing our famed coffee and for matinée teas. Room was made for cloakrooms and lavatories. On first nights this foyer would become packed with 'gowns' and 'tails' and on sunny evenings many would adjourn to the street, coffee-cup in hand, to the delight of the tenement wits. In the basement, at the opposite end to the Green-Room, was a large old-fashioned iron cooking-stove with ovens which burned a lovely comforting fire in winter. At right angles to it we placed two 'property' high-backed pub benches from the set for *Nan*. This nook was where management gathered with artistes in their make-up when off-stage, in intervals, and notably on Saturdays between matinée and evening performances. Mrs. Franklin or Mrs. Doddington served tea with home-baked scones. And here Edith Evans unwittingly christened this book. "I don't know what comes over you all up here . . . it's a mania . . . a MANIA!"

CANTICLES OF HISTORY

with interpolations
*in Six Scenes
and Finale*

Scene I: 1920

On the 15th September, 1920, the Everyman Theatre opened for its first performance. As the first new theatre in London for many years, it was a social occasion. In front of the curtain, 'all mink and diamonds', it seemed smooth and easy: behind the curtain, all snags and despair. The play was *The Bonds of Interest* by the Spanish dramatist Jacinto Benavente that had been a success in translation in America. Frightening problems accumulated throughout the day, at the last minute, and even through the performance.

First, during the afternoon, was a threat of a writ barring the performance, pending settlement of a dispute between the American and the English translators of the play, both claiming performing rights. A slip had to be hurriedly printed and inserted in the programmes. Next and worse: the workshop and stage staff had been busy right through the previous night; all the day practically without stop; and, near exhaustion, were struggling to finish the scene settings in time. Before the doors were to open for the audience I took a last look round. A large *flat* with a heavy doorway under an iron-grilled window 'in the Spanish manner' was angled across the stage, supported by one man in front while another prepared to fix the brace at the back. With ten minutes to go, the stage manager asked whether the men could take the time for a quick drink. Permission given, they were in the street in a flash. As the stage manager started to close the velvet front-curtains the built piece, left untended, swayed gently twice then crashed. A corner, catching the velvets, ripped a seven-foot tear across the top. "Ladders—Wardrobe-Mistress—needles and thread—a strip of sail-cloth!" . . . "Get the men back!" I tore off my tail-coat, pulled on a boiler-suit and set to with the wardrobe women stitching furiously while a very subdued crew of men re-erected the scene in gloomy silence.

Finished, at last! The audience crowding in, a little impatient

at the delay. The stage manager's last check-round in lowered
voice. Two minutes to go. First Gong and Foyer Bells. On-stage
and off-stage some thirty figures quivering in every nerve. Second
Gong and House-lights. A long deep breath from everyone.
Third Gong and Curtain Up!

Twenty minutes late! The Everyman is launched. Launched!
But into rough seas and a horrifying third snag. Listening to the
dialogue and waiting for the first response from the audience, I
noticed that the scene crash had caused one of the curtain draw-
lines to jump its track and fifteen feet of rope was snarled up like
a serpent in death throes. The front curtains would not be able to
be closed at the act-end! The incident serves to introduce Martin,
one of the most loyal of Everymaniacs. At that time he was
assistant-electrician but later at sundry times he became caretaker,
boilerman, cleaner-in-charge: in fact anything that no one else
could or would do, Martin did. He had been to sea in sail and had
rigged all our over-stage tackle. Now, passing a satisfied eye over
his own handiwork, he had seen the snarled rope and was already
inching outward along a steel girder to reach it. Hanging upside-
down, his feet clasped over the steel joist, he edged out over the
brightly lit stage. At any moment it seemed his boiler-suited figure
might land spread-eagled among the gaily caparisoned characters
twenty feet below. One of them sword half-drawn, caught sight
of the hanging face; muttered a word not in the script and ram-
med his sword deep into its scabbard. Martin, having freed the
rope, slid back onto the electrician's perch, his satisfied grin like
a white bar across his sweating face.

Then yet a fourth snag. The stage was reached by two narrow
spiral iron staircases in the back corners. The ladies' costumes
were Velasquez period. At dress-rehearsals they all gathered in
the auditorium to see the set before we started and from there
went up on stage. When they were called for entrance on the first
night the hooped skirts would not go up the narrow iron stairs.
Off the skirts had to come: the artistes sprinted upstairs in their
underthings and dived into the dresses as they were rushed in
through the stage door. Those who had ignored my insistence
that period dresses must always be worn with the period 'beneaths'
had a very shame-faced stair-climb.

The play was a costume comedy with dialogue of wit and
sparkle. The gay-coloured costumes, from designs by John

Garside, and the brightly-lit white scenery were such a contrast to anything in the depressed post-war theatre that the audience responded rapturously. After many curtain calls for the company I was demanded by name. Still in the boiler-suit, white bow-tie askew, I went hesitantly on stage to apologise for the delays and the raggedness. That fortuitous boiler-suit, I believe, disarmed impending criticism. It seemed to announce "No airs and graces here: in spite of shortcomings, we are in this seriously". Dressing-rooms and corridors were packed with a throng of congratulatory friends of the company. I felt an undernote of almost surprised relief. I went to thank the stage crew for the splendid effort they had made. Then, standing in the middle of the darkened stage, looking up the auditorium slope, I thought: "So far! But not good enough! Excuses won't make success. What will the Press say in the morning?" Surprisingly the notices, though guarded, were favorable. A comedy, almost farce, must go with a swing and there had been little swing, many creakings. But on the whole the reception was good, and there was definitely a genuine welcome to the venture.

To follow the opening production the plays announced for the three months until Christmas were: *The Tragedy of Nan* by John Masefield; *You Never Can Tell* by Bernard Shaw; *The Foundations* and *The Little Man* by John Galsworthy; *The Melting Pot* by Israel Zangwill; *The Honeymoon* by Arnold Bennett; and *Romeo and Juliet* by Shakespeare. There is little of the experimental in this list although in the ambience of time it seemed adventurous. The intent was to bring back to the London stage established English authors who had been driven from the theatre by the war-time hysteria, and to show that our choice of plays would be in the tradition of dramatic literature and not bedroom farce or leg-show. At that time few English authors, old or new, were writing for the theatre but it was expected, if we showed there was in London at least one management prepared to risk plays of substance and present them with fully professional standards, that writers would return to the play-form and scripts would flow to the theatre.

Masefield's *Nan* was remarkably well received. Several members of the company had played in it in provincial theatres before the war and rehearsals went well; it requires only one set and no scene change. Press notices reported the performance "went well and smoothly". It brought back into the theatre a poetical quality that people were thirsting for after the war-time grim rejection. Zangwill's *The Melting Pot* had relevance to conditions in America and was a success there, but although the cast received good notices the play was felt to be out of date, "preachy and pontifical". Of Galsworthy's *Foundations* and Arnold Bennett's *The Honeymoon* it can only be said that although the performances got excellent notices the London playgoer showed little interest. The good notices, however, resulted in an invitation to present these productions in Manchester and in Harrogate for a three weeks run. *Romeo and Juliet* got a very mixed reception from the critics. There was high praise for Muriel Pratt's Juliet, for Nicholas Hannen's Romeo, and for Brember Wills's Friar. But there were very bad scene-change delays on the first night and a late finish, causing the critics, who still had to make the long journey from Hampstead to Fleet Street, to feel unkindly disposed. Later in the week when scene-changing had been smoothed out the notices were better. But we were not yet sufficiently a stage-team to cope with the special difficulties of a Shakespearean production (*Illus. 5*).

Generally the lesser critics tended to fill their space with complaints that the plays were not new and with snappy comments on shortcomings such as the late start, the lengthy scene-change, and lighting mistakes. The more knowledgeable critics on established papers soon gave much more space to considered notices and, as we overcame our earlier faults and the company got into stride, their notices became more appreciative and welcoming. Without the understanding support of the major dailies the venture might well have died before the year end. It may be true that even a good notice cannot ensure success for a play but certainly a bad one can kill it in a space of days. One well-known school that had arranged to take a large block of seats for a matinée of *Romeo and Juliet* asked us to release them because the pupils reported their parents, having read certain paragraphs, judged the performance must be so bad that they would not give their money for the tickets.

The outstanding success was Bernard Shaw's *You Never Can Tell*. There were almost full houses for every performance including matinées. This was to have a profound influence on the whole future of the Everyman.

opposite: Illus. 7 The permanent Shakespeare set
(See page 51)   *Author's photograph*

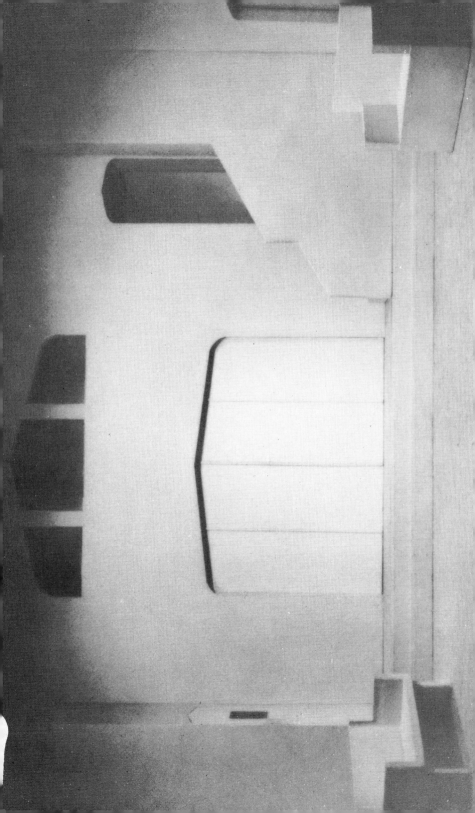

For the Christmas period the Everyman must offer entertainment very different from the mixture of music-hall slapstick and false sentiment that, called pantomime, was London's usual fare. For the matinées *Through the Crack*, a play for children, by Algernon Blackwood and Violet Pearn, was chosen. Music for this had been composed by a member of the company, Laurence Hanray, with some additional songs by Harold Scott, another member, and a small orchestra was gathered. A mass of toys, generously given by the Lord Roberts Workshop to be used on the stage, were raffled at the end of the run on free tickets issued with every programme sold. The play had a long cast and a number of additions were made to the company including a very attractive *star* in Renée Mayer. The production was a complete success, played to full houses, and was asked for in the following year.

At the evening performances for the regular audience I had decided to present *A Nativity Play* arranged from the York and Coventry mediaeval cycles by Professor E. K. Chambers, with music arranged by Charles Kennedy-Scott. For this the soloist was Lady Maud Warrender who with a small choir sang the ancient carols off-stage. These simple 14th-century re-tellings of Bible stories as natural occurrences of daily life, unaffected and sincere, even including the rollicking songs of the Shepherds, celebrating birth, made a moving effect. Critics and audiences were enthralled. The Prologue was spoken by no less than Ellen Terry. She was then 74 yet the critics wrote of the rich quality of her voice and the clarity of her speaking. For me it was memorable as the first of two occasions when that gracious lady was, though briefly, a member of my company (*Illus.* 8).

With these Christmas productions the attempt at true repertory at the Everyman was abandoned. The word *repertory* had been so misused in England that it is well to clarify the Everyman use of it, and our later modifications. In the continental theatre, repertory indicated that a different play would be performed each night of the week (including Sundays) and that when audience-interest slackened the number of appearances of any play would be correspondingly reduced until eventually it might be dropped from the lists for a period but would be stored and could be brought forward again to meet renewed interest. This system had never been adopted in London. Outside London, repertory was used

opposite: Illus. 8 Ellen Terry as Prologue in *The Nativity Play*. Christmas 1920
Illus. 9 Ellen Terry in the garden of the cottage at Smallhythe with the author's daughter. 1921 (See page 37)

to describe the few theatres in provincial cities with semi-perm-anent companies that put on a different play every week, mostly copies of London successes. These were not true repertory but short-run weekly schemes. Their companies had only five days to prepare each play and they had developed a technique by which they gave quite creditable performances of that type of play but only a public starved of theatre could be satisfied with the results. The famous Dublin Abbey Theatre; Miss Horniman's Gaiety Theatre in Manchester; Sir Barry Jackson's beautiful Repertory Theatre in Birmingham had variations on this system and gave performances fully justifying their repute.

There was no equivalent in, or near, London where the firmly established system was the long-run *star* production that continued for months, in some cases for years, until all interest in the play was exhausted or the *star* broke under the strain. The accepted principle of London managements was that if any play could be kept on for six weeks it would prove to be a success and run for a year. For the most part they were justified in their belief, but many a good play has died because its backers had not the resources to meet heavy weekly shortages entailed by half-empty auditoriums and costly advertising.

The Everyman had not the resources of working-room, storage-space, staff, nor capital to sink in scenery and properties, to adopt the full-scale continental practice. A compromise that kept close to true repertory working was adopted. On a rota system two plays would be performed in each week for three days each by the same company of artistes. Thus on the opening night the ensuing production was due in four days (one being Sunday and dress rehearsal). It would run for three nights and be replaced by the third play on the announced list. These three would alternate in three-day periods for a month until the fourth play was ready. This would replace the least successful of the group for the ensuing month during which the fifth would be prepared. The company would be permanent and an artiste might be playing a leading part in one play in the week and a small part in the other, or might be studying for a long or difficult part in a play in rehearsal. The system worked well in the theatre, and after some weeks was warmly welcomed by the company. But not by the public. Most London playgoers were accustomed to wait until a play had been running for a week or two before bestirring themselves to keep up with the Joneses and "go West" to see it. The Everyman could count on its regulars but needed also bookings by other playgoers. There was no passing traffic at Hampstead. In the West End, failing to get into a play of choice in Shaftesbury Avenue, one could hurry to half a dozen other theatres within a stone-throw; but it took half an hour to get to Hampstead. The weary tube journey, finishing with the deepest and slowest tube lift in all London, called for real courage and determination. The alternative, taxis, at that time had almost to be bribed to grind up Fitzjohn's Avenue or Haverstock Hill. The Everyman, in fact, had fallen between proverbial stools. It could count neither on the patronage of the Garden Suburb nor the artistic consciousness of Hampstead, nor could it expect casual entertainment-seekers from around Piccadilly Circus.

With the Christmas plays we had arrived at the end of our promised experimental three months and it was obviously occasion for a realistic survey of results and of lessons learned from our errors and blunders. One of the first was that the early assumption, encouraged by Shaw and Galsworthy, that Hampstead would provide the steady nucleus of an audience was completely exploded. A postal-advice service of plays and dates was being developed and the addresses proved that the audiences came from all parts of London but Hampstead residents provided quite a small proportion of seat bookings. Our necessarily limited press and poster advertising was quite inadequate to cover all areas. We could afford only minimum space in a selected number of papers and journals; our tube and bus poster positions had to be restricted to a hundred for the whole of London.

Even our regular supporters started to press for longer consecutive 'runs'. Dramatic critics and paragraphists urged it. So when eventually an enquirer at the box office, being told that the play that night was *You Never Can Tell*, said, "Good gracious! Don't they even tell you?", we deferred to London's prejudice and decided that true repertory must be abandoned. Another drastic lesson was that while we could lose as much as £300 in a week with a play that flopped, we could never make more than £50 at the most with a success. Furthermore, it was clear that although artistes had given most generously of spirit, time and ability at minimal salaries (and this might be accepted through a consolidation period) salary rates would have to be improved at some not too future date. These and other problems were fully discussed by the Board members. No one wanted to abandon the venture and, although with much anxiety, it was decided to undertake a further three months. Some modifications were suggested but not, at any time, in the play selection. Also those members who were knowledgeable on theatre supported my determination that the Everyman should not succumb to the provincial play-per-week practice. Rough and ready as some of our early performances had been, our sights were firmly set on productions which would eventually challenge comparison with any theatre. From this, and the corollary that a minimum of three weeks preparation for each play was essential, the three-week-run system evolved.

The main problem was, of course, general finance. It was recognised that endowment in some form must eventually be found; but there was at that time no Arts Council. Support for the Arts from public money was considered a joke in the worst of taste. As the financial struggle became known and appeals were made, the press gave sympathetic and even anxious publicity. A fund of £4,000 was asked for. As one result I received a telephone call from a lady entirely unknown to any of us. This was the Countess Bubna who offered to donate half the amount subject to other supporters contributing the balance. Through individual letters and circulars, "Friends of the Everyman" were asked to take up Debentures of £500 each and so enable us to accept the Countess's offer. Shortly we had promises of £1,250 from supporters, including the lessor, Mr. Frank G. Foster, who had already generously given substantial sums. On being told of this, the Countess generously offered to give also the balance of £750 in addition to her first £2,000.

This munificent gift placed the theatre for the first time on a sound capital basis and a magic wave of relief carried us through to the spring season. Before this some domestic adjustments had been made, including the departure of two or three artistes whose spirit was not that of the majority. The three-week run system was developed and later a further small modification was introduced. The theatre was closed on the Monday of each production week and the dress-rehearsal was taken as a private performance. This had many advantages; it gave the artistes a valuable break to slough-off one play and come freshly to the new, and it gave the workshop and stage staff time to make the scenery change-over without working all of one night. Productions for which there was still box-office enquiry at the end of the allotted three weeks were reserved in cold-storage and formed the nucleus of the special Seasons which became the framework of our presentations.

One major change also was made at Christmas in the administration of the theatre which was to lead to near disaster. It was a customary belief that no artiste, even though not long-haired, could be a practical business man and this belief was very strongly held by Mr. Foster. He now insisted on the appointment of a Finance Controller to be in charge of all the business-managerial side and to ensure that the new capital would be skilfully handled. There had been coming about the theatre such a professional man interested in one of the company (whom he later married). Foster was greatly impressed by him and now stipulated that he be appointed to the new position. Admittedly I was not altogether happy that so important and influential a post should be held by a stranger to our ways. It was urged, however, that I "had too much on my shoulders", which was true, and that it would be to the advantage of the whole if the artistic and the business departments were separated. It is true also that the proposal had some attraction for me as it would relieve me of much detail and day-to-day worry and free me to work out the policy adjustments that had been decided on.

In discussion at a meeting of the Board members I pointed out that the finances were in such satisfactory state as they had never been before. Mr. Foster in turn said, correctly, that he had already invested a lot of money and still had much at risk. In agreeing finally to the change, I stipulated that all cheques drawn on the company's bank account must bear my signature as well as that of the Controller. He in his turn stipulated that his name should not appear on the programmes as Business Manager. Other changes were made, which included the winding-up of the original company and by which Foster acquired the lease of the theatre as security for his contributions. At first the arrangement seemed to work well with only occasional frictions, but later when I made requests for information about the financial side I was fobbed off and asked to restrict myself to the artistic side. I complained to Mr. Foster about this but the suggestion was made that I was merely showing jealousy. The final result will appear later.

Scene II: 1921

To include *You Never Can Tell* in our opening Season had been quite a risk. During the first world war Shaw had been extravagantly abused: his *New Statesman* supplement *The Truth about the War* had infuriated the super-patriots and even by 1920 he had still not been fully accepted back into the comity. But the audience enthusiasm for *You Never Can Tell* seemed a clear pointer to present more of his plays. For the Spring of 1921 a Shaw Season was announced, to include: *You Never Can Tell* (repeat), *Candida, The Doctor's Dilemma, Man and Superman, Major Barbara*, and a Triple Bill with *The Shewing-up of Blanco Posnet, How he lied to her Husband* and *The Dark Lady of the Sonnets*. Most of these plays had not been performed since the original Vedrenne-Barker productions in 1904/6. Amongst the more knowledgeable and enthusiastic supporters who had gathered round the theatre were three women friends who, on closer acquaintance, we christened "The Three Musketeers": they all wore the voluminous black *capa* of Italian cavalry officers, recently acquired on a visit to Italy, and large floppy black hats. These were Miss Edith Craig, Miss Christopher St. John and Miss Clare Atwood.

The production of *Romeo and Juliet* in the previous year in repertoire conditions had required an assistant producer: I had asked Miss Craig to rehearse the general crowd-movement and the fights, and most convincing and dramatic she made them. I now asked her to undertake the whole of the next season's productions under an arrangement that should be announced and printed in programmes as "The Play produced by Miss Edith Craig under the General Direction of Norman MacDermott". I should cast the plays, in consultation with her, design the settings and lighting, and have general supervision on important matters. Miss Craig not only accepted this very unusual arrangement but most loyally carried it into practice during the course of our association. I found her delightful to work with, easy, good-humoured and loyal. The Everyman, and even more myself, owe her a deep gratitude for the richness of spirit that she brought to this difficult assignment.

During this Season the stimulus of Shaw's thought and the wit of his dialogue was an exciting discovery to the younger play-goers and to the older a welcome opportunity to renew their enjoyment. The response of the critics in general can be summed up by one who wrote: "How pleasant it is to see a good comedy... something so rare on the London stage that we almost forgot what it looks and sounds like and when one actually presents itself to the sight and hearing it brings with it a certain shock of surprise and amazement." And another: ". . . so enthusiastic was the reception that one found it difficult to avoid the impression that the vast majority of the audience were listening to the play for the first time." Several of the critics were certainly seeing them for their first time. Some found it still difficult to write of the author without war-time prejudice but the standard of the per-formances won over practically all. "The acting throughout was extremely good." "Muriel Pratt scores something of a triumph." "Dorothy Massingham's Barbara . . . had a spiritual quality that lifts it far above the average merely clever performance", and, "You were able to perceive more clearly than at the original pro-duction what is the true dramatic conflict of the play." "In no play now on the West-End stage is the level of acting quite so high."

Blanco Posnet had been under censorship since it was written in 1909. This was its first public presentation in London and accordingly something of an occasion with a very distinguished audience, including Ellen Terry. As Blanco, Brember Wills "gave a remarkable performance" . . . "a sense of nervous apprehension at the mysterious acts of God". Of Felix Aylmer, three different critics used the one word "Perfect". "The acting is a great triumph for the Everyman Theatre and will undoubtedly enhance the high reputation which this talented company has secured." An occasion of some note was a performance of the complete *Man and Superman* with Nicholas Hannen playing the long scene in Hell. This was given on a Sunday evening for members of the 'Friends of the Everyman'. Just before dress-rehearsal of *Candida*, due on a Sunday, Nicholas Hannen completely lost his voice. We were almost in despair because his performance as Marjoribanks promised to be outstanding. We did not run to the luxury of understudies and a switch-round of cast was not practicable. Rumour reached us that the part was being played in Miss Lena Ashwell's touring company by a "promising young man". Late on Saturday afternoon a car was hurriedly ordered and Edith Craig and I set off for a remote and depressing suburban Hall, one of those to which Miss Ashwell so courageously took plays of merit. The promising young man was Leslie Banks. Here, without question, was an actor whose promise was a reality. We arranged for him to rehearse over the weekend and he played the part at the Everyman on the Monday. Hannen recovered his voice in a day or two and returned to his part. Nevertheless I recruited Banks as a permanent member of the company. He next played three small parts in *The Doctor's Dilemma* (Redpenny, Newspaper-man and a Waiter) thus 'shoe-horning' into our ways. He was in the company for two years and his most notable performance was as Benny with Miss Jean Cadell in Eugene O'Neill's *Diff'rent*, of which we made the first production in England.

Rumour, on another occasion, told of a beautiful young actress who was being wasted in a company at Grimsby. I hurried to that town of unsalubrious odour and saw a performance. Beautiful indeed she was but could not act, and, as I judged, never would be able to. However, I had compensation for the journey because I noted one real actor in the play and brought back with me that most able character actor George Merritt as another recruit to *Everymania*, who later gave a most notable performance as the Judge in *The Mask and the Face*. Another such discovery was Raymond Massey, an unknown amateur from Canada, who had his first part in England at the Everyman and was in the company for several years. It was by such explorations of touring and provincial companies and giving young unknowns their first chance on a London stage, and by offering well-established West-End players interesting parts in plays of real merit, that I was able to maintain the strength of the company even at our modest salaries.

The Shaw Season was an unqualified success. Some critics advocated the establishment of a permanent Shaw repertory. St. John Ervine suggested that the name *Everyman* would have to be changed to *One-Man*. To adopt such a policy would have been a serious blunder. After a year or two we should exhaust the poten-tial audience; dissipate the regular support we were trying to build; and cease experimental play selection which, as the result proved, would have deprived the theatre of its endowment by profits on West-End transfers. Some change seemed desirable, and for the last production before closing for the summer a completely different type of entertainment was staged called *The Pedlar's Basket*. On a short visit to Paris to see Copeau's renowned Vieux Colombier Theatre I had also seen the Russian *Chauve Souris* of Nikita Balieff with great enjoyment and felt that a similar concoction would provide acceptable light entertainment for our kind of audience. Built up mainly of one-act plays it would give opportunity to introduce new authors, particularly the important American Eugene O'Neill, whose work was entirely unknown in England. Interspersed with an operetta, other unusual musical items and some dance items it would be Variety of a different kind. Clarence Raybould undertook the musical arrangements; Marie Rambert danced the special items; John Goss was the singer. It had a number of colourful and amusing settings. The Molière, which I had copied from Copeau's production, amused me greatly but was a grim failure and had to be replaced quickly with an alternative item.

The play by Eugene O'Neill was *In the Zone* and his first production in Europe. It was my first clash with censorship. I had been eager to introduce this new American playwright to London; his plays were not known and could not be bought here but someone from the 'Little Theatre Movement' had brought me a copy of his first published volume *The Moon of the Carribees*. I wrote to O'Neill but he was hesitant about granting performing rights having had bad reports of the London theatre. After some correspondence he agreed that I might do *In the Zone* and others would depend on the reports of our production.

Over *In the Zone* I was summoned to St. James's and faced with a schedule of cuts that would have turned every tough sailor in the Fo'c'sle into a supplicant for Holy Orders. "God blarst you" occurred nineteen times and must be reduced to five. "Bloody" must be deleted entirely. I decided this was an occasion for an outright no-bar fight. First I reasoned, pointing out that men in an armaments-carrying ship and in the war-zone under submarine threat would be screwed-tense and using their worst language; that in the play it was, in fact, used with restraint to produce its effect of character; that, severely modified as proposed, the veracity would be lost and no audience would accept the play. I added that the author would certainly not agree to such whole-sale excisions. Finally I contended that this was no way to treat either an author of outstanding importance or my 'congregation' of intelligent people which was not a Girls' School. I reminded that "Bloody" had been made respectable by Mrs. Patrick Campbell in *Pygmalion* and that "Bloody" was being spoken at that very time in Lord Dunsany's *If* at the Ambassadors Theatre. After this discussion the number of permissible "God blarst yous" was raised to eleven.

I refused to make any other cuts and said I would produce the play, licence or no licence. This was received with polite disbelief until I said that I had a membership of over 2,000 in the 'Friends of the Everyman' and could run the play for a fortnight on a membership basis, and would then run it for a third week free of admission charge to the general public. At this I was invited to consider that renewal of my special theatre Licence could be resisted at the next renewal date.

Meantime, glancing down the list of deletions to be made I realised that one expletive, so offensive that even I had noted it in my production script for deletion, had been missed by the Reader and was not endorsed on the Licence. This gave me the idea of how best to cope with the situation. So I suddenly capitulated and said I would accept the Licence with the required deletions. With relief they gave me the Licence and showed me out.

On the First-Night I went in front of the Curtain. I told the audience I felt guilty to be taking their money by giving them only part of the play, as the Lord Chamberlain had cut so much of it out. In compensation I had decided to read to them the cuts demanded. I told them of the total deletion of "Bloody" and of the cuts in permitted "God blarst you" which had been considerably raised to eleven. On the other hand, I said, the Censor had left in an expletive which I thought much more offensive. And gave it—"Christ blind you". There was delighted laughter and cheering. Bernard Shaw was in the audience and praised my 'cheek'. Next day the press gave us much more column space than usual.

The production of *The Pedlar's Basket* was a gratifying success and so enthusiastically received that it brought an invitation from Mr. Donald Calthrop to present three one-act plays at the

Queen's Theatre in Shaftesbury Avenue. This was a real boost to prestige and also enabled me to keep the company together during July and August when, according to plan, the Everyman was to be closed.

We seemed 'set fair': a real dent had been made in the complacency of the West-End theatre and permanent success seemed within grasp. Then, out of this sunny sky, a bomb fell. On a Friday morning I was called out of rehearsal to take an urgent telephone call from the Finance Controller. He explained that he was "detained on a case in Court", and could not get up to the theatre during the day, but as the company salary cheques were all made out, he asked me to sign these and have them issued during the evening, as is theatre custom. He would telephone the Bank Manager and arrange to add his own signature in the following week as they were paid in. Unsuspectingly, not being a practical businessman, I did so. On Saturday morning a distressed member of the company came and told me that he had taken his cheque to the Bank and payment had been refused. I telephoned to the Bank Manager and was told there was no money in our account to meet any payments. It seemed inexplicable. In addition to the donated sum of £4,000 there had been a steady flow of income from almost full houses for the Shaw plays. Members of the company who had put their cheques through their own Banks were blissfully unaware although by evening the news was round and from one or two there were threats not to play that night; but the community spirit of the majority, loyalty to the Everyman on the part of some and to myself from others, sent up the curtain.

That evening I took possession of the business office and commenced an investigation of the books and records with the help of my secretary, Miss Kent. All Saturday night we worked without break except for the tea or coffee brought to us from time to time by the caretaker, the invaluable Martin in another of his roles. By Sunday afternoon the job was done and I was faced with a list of unpaid liabilities totalling over £3,000. I telephoned Mr. Foster in Yorkshire. My story was not believed, but on my emphatic insistence he agreed to come down on the following day. Both the Fosters, father and son, arrived in the afternoon and there was a tense and uncomfortable hour in my office. They at first refused to accept my report and again accused me of jealousy and an attempt to oust the Finance Controller but I had spent the morning interviewing or telephoning most of the creditors on my list and I knew my story was substantially correct. I demanded an immediate full Board enquiry and was told that if I persisted it meant that "one of us would have to go". I said I would attach my conditional resignation to my Report. The Finance Controller had not come near the theatre that day and a peremptory call to him was sent to attend a meeting of the Board. The meeting was held on Wednesday afternoon. Present were both Fosters, the Finance Controller, and three or four of the Board, all that could be got together in the time. I told my story and tabled a copy of my Report and the list of liabilities. There was no explanation from the office of the Finance Controller. The shock to the Fosters and to the Board members was certainly not less than to myself.

The Everyman never fully recovered from this set-back. The ensuing years became a period of unending struggle to pay off liabilities, while unsuccessful plays, good or bad, created more. The liabilities included rent due to Mr. Foster, trading debts and authors' royalties. Shaw had never complained to me, but some £450 was overdue to him and on all future productions of his plays at the Everyman, we had to pay 2½ per cent additional royalty until the amount was cleared. It was painfully obvious that there was necessity for a second and even more serious reappraisal. All the signs pointed to abandoning the struggle and terminating the theatre. But I was obstinate. I argued with Foster; I pleaded with him on the evidence of the Shaw Season box-office returns and to the delighted laughter of the audience that we could hear through the observation window in my office. I outlined proposals for an International Season of plays from many countries for which I had secured the official support of the League of Nations. I argued that the press and other supporters would rally to our help. Eventually, he most sportingly agreed to partner me on one other attempt, to a definite limit of £1,500.

While awaiting the opening date of the transfer to the Queen's Theatre, the company put on some performances of Ibsen's *A Doll's House* and then duly transferred for the agreed four weeks with *A Farewell Supper* by Arthur Schnitzler, *The Dark Lady of the Sonnets* and *The Shewing-up of Blanco Posnet* by Bernard Shaw. August that year was overpoweringly hot and several theatres closed for lack of audience. The Queen's was never packed, and although one-act plays were traditionally unpopular in the West End, there were good enough houses to satisfy both Calthrop and myself. During the Season in April we had marked the Shakespeare Birthday Anniversary with a matinée and evening performance of a series of scenes from the plays with a considerably augmented company including Ellen Terry playing Portia in the trial scene from *The Merchant of Venice*. This was Miss Terry's last appearance on the public stage.

I needed time to think and time for detail planning of renewed effort in the Autumn. Edith Craig suggested I should take the small cottage belonging to her mother at Smallhythe: not the Farmhouse (which was her residence and let at that time to some American visitors) but across the road from it. I gladly agreed. With my wife and infant daughter, in the small leafy garden, London and struggle seemed blissfully distant. One day Miss Craig telephoned to say that her mother found the urban heat intolerable: would we have her to stay for the weekend? We were appalled, even terrified, at the thought of entertaining so great a person. On Friday afternoon, feeling dwarf-size, I set out to Tenterden station in the small governess car, drawn by an aged and practically comatose pony, to meet our guest. On the return, whether my nervousness communicated through the reins or merely to show it was in no awe of the great, the pony, after about a mile of ambling along, suddenly bolted. In a lather, it stopped as suddenly at the cottage gate. "Well ... here we are", said Ellen Terry quietly. No reprimand for me; or for the pony: just gentle relief at survival. And again, as with the boiler-suit, the situation was saved. Miss Terry 'adopted' the baby at once and for most of the weekend played most divinely as Nanny. This weekend remains one of the most enchanting incidents of my life (*Illus 9*).

In early September we returned to London and active preparation for the International Season. This was announced as "Under the Patronage of the League of Nations Union". Apart from "two dull and tedious" (press quote) addresses on the opening night by prominent officials of the League, the patronage proved to be in reverse. No support of any sort was given by the League whereas the theatre showed its posters, distributed its literature, and provided a useful propaganda outlet when the League was still struggling to birth. The Season was international in that plays were selected to make known the work of authors from Great Britain, America, Germany, Scandinavia, France and Ireland. The first programme was given to America and included, with the amusing trifle *Suppressed Desires* by Susan Glaspell, *Diff'rent* by Eugene O'Neill with whose one-act play *In the Zone* we had first made him known in England. *Diff'rent* was immediately applauded by the critics as the work of a major dramatist. The acting of Jean Cadell and of Leslie Banks received unlimited praise. Looking back over the press reception, this production stands out as a milestone on our progress to critical acceptance.

The second programme was German. The play was *The Race with the Shadow* by a new writer, Wilhelm von Scholz, translated by Graham and Tristan Rawson. I had been urged to give an opening to a Russian refugee, Theodore Komisarjevsky, who had been Director and Producer at State Theatres in Petrograd and Moscow but in London had not had any opportunity except for a performance of a Chekhov one-act at an Exhibition. I offered him the opportunity to produce the German play. Neither play nor performance made much of a mark, but better followed. The Scandinavian Bill gave the appropriate opportunity to present Ibsen and I had selected *John Gabriel Borkman*. I wanted to produce this myself but Komisarjevsky urged me to let him do it and a very impressive performance he obtained. Although it had a mixed reception from the critics I consider it one of the outstanding productions of the Everyman. Franklin Dyall, who had been in both casts, gave a wicked parody of rehearsals: "You take the cop—you do not speak. You put in one teaspoon sugar—you do not speak. You stir the tea—still you do not speak. You put down the cop—THEN you speak and it ees significant."

The English programme was made up of four plays by Lord Dunsany: *Cheeso, The Tents of the Arabs, A Night at an Inn* and *The Lost Silk Hat*. Trifling, colourful and delighting the audiences, but by the critics not thought important enough for the standard that by this time they expected of the Everyman. A very pleasant memory remains, however, of J. H. Roberts and Harold Scott sitting on the doorstep of a London mansion arguing over the significance of a tile hat that had been left inside. There was an amusing tussle between Lord Dunsany, who was very tall, and our stage-manager, George Carr, who was very small. We had just acquired, with great pride, a very wide mahogany board and fixed it along the whole front of the stage to add éclat. It was lovingly polished many times a day. Dunsany came to some rehearsals and gave offence, not only by sitting in the front row of the stalls, but by stretching out his long legs and planting his feet on the mahogany. Sometimes he was in uniform and wore spurs. The stage-manager and his crew were ready to defend their board against the whole British Army but Dunsany would take no hints. As a solution the master-carpenter proposed taking out the front row of the stalls, before the next rehearsal. Dunsany arrived, again sat in the new front row, merely hunched a bit lower, and still his feet reached the mahogany making a long scratch. The following day the little stage-manager sat on the scratch facing the stalls and glared hard at Dunsany who could not very well put his feet on Carr's lap. A rather edgy rehearsal ensued.

Ireland was represented by the Abbey Theatre Players with Synge's *The Shadow of the Glen; The Building Fund* by William Boyle, and *Mixed Marriage* by St. John Ervine. The Irish plays were restricted to daily matinées until mid-January so that over the Christmas period we could again show lighter entertainment, with music. *Prunella* by Granville Barker and Laurence Housman with Joseph Moorat's music was chosen, and Milton Rosmer gave a very moving performance as Pierrot as also did Hazel Jones in the name part. With *Mixed Marriage* the Abbey Company was restored to evening performances and closed the International Season.

At the end of the year when discussing the position with Mr. Foster he regretted he could not risk any further financial liability and he finally withdrew from all association with the theatre except as landlord holding the lease of the building which he would rent to me at the same figure as it had been leased to the Company: £10 per week. There were now no Councillors, no Board-Members, no Partners. This left me with the full responsibility and the financial liability: whether to continue or to close-down was entirely my decision. I turned for advice to the very helpful Bank Manager. After long and detailed discussion he suggested that I should seek enough working capital to test the result of one more Season and added half-jokingly, "When in doubt—play Shaw". For the next four years I was entirely on my own.

Scene III: 1922

In January 1922 the second Shaw Season was announced and duly opened in mid-February after the end of the International Season. The plays to be given were: *Fanny's First Play*; *Arms and the Man*; *Getting Married*; *Misalliance*; *You Never Can Tell* (repeat); *Candida* (repeat); and, as a later addition, *Widowers' Houses*. Having watched several producers in the Everyman, participated in their work, selected the casts, designed the sets and lighting, and generally supervised with intent that each play should have an Everyman hallmark, I felt that now I had something to add and I decided that I was ready to produce most of the plays myself.

In the following months I was most fortunate in that Shaw began to take a much closer interest and came to some rehearsals. He would ring up and ask what state the rehearsals had reached; whether the moves were settled and whether the company had "got rid of their books yet"? Then he would come up to the theatre two or three mornings spread over the final ten days. He would sit silent, well back in the auditorium; sometimes I would not know he was there until suddenly that bright voice with its endearing Dublin slant would break in with "No. . . . No. . . . It's not like that at ahl." He would jump from his seat, hurry down the aisle, spring onto the stage, and for the next ten minutes or so he would himself act every character in the scene he had stopped, illuminating it to the delight of us all. Never was anyone reproved or snubbed; always corrections were given in so kindly a way with unfailing consideration. Then equally suddenly he would turn self-conscious, pull awkwardly at his collar, mutter apologetically, dive off the stage and return to his seat. We felt he was happy. It was in these interludes that we grew to know him and admiration turned to affection for the un-public man.

Successful acting of Shaw is far from as easy as a reading of the plays might suggest. In some respects they are easy to rehearse because the stage-movements have already been worked out by the author during writing, and the published editions are all printed from prompt-books, made after the original productions. They are even not difficult, as reputed, but they are different, and this difference has to be learned. The difference with Shaw arises because an unusual style of playing has to be found. While lines are spoken with convincing seriousness the audience must be given a clue to the inherent irony. The conventional well-made comedy of the commercial theatre was carried by one, or perhaps two, particularly skilled and experienced artistes. The rest of the company served for little more than to provide linking information, feed the principals, and fill the stage between high spots. This is not so with Shaw. There are no leading parts in the usual sense; every character must make a convincing contribution to the whole. This calls for a much more cogent study of the script. In the acting realism or naturalism is not sufficient: there is an overtone that must be captured. A controlled exaggeration, even an extravagance, is an essential ingredient. Artistes can find it very difficult to achieve this without any trace of 'hamming'. To have the same company of artistes playing together in a sequence of the plays over a period of months was invaluable and was the basis of our success. Critics wrote "at the Everyman they seem to have found the knack of acting Shaw".

Several of the earlier plays require some really awkward props. A heavy, working dentist's chair; a portable Turkish bath; an easily negotiable wheeled-chair; a racing motor-car. These caused us both trouble and amusement. For *Man and Superman* we had secured the loan of a powerful-looking car with an exceptionally long body. Very impressive it looked during the act; but there was no room on either side of our stage to park it during the other acts. The invaluable Martin rigged tackle to the back axle and pulleys on the roof-girders: "heave-ho" and the car hung ignominiously, radiator down, behind the Sierra Nevada. It pleased us that the Sierra Nevada scene got special praise from some critics.

I first met Shaw during a Fabian weekend conference in a country house in the English Lake District where were staying also the Webbs, Graham Wallas, Philip Guedalla and others. Shaw spoke comparatively little during the discussions but after dinner, when we drifted out to sit on the terrace to enjoy the evening sky and the quietness broken only by the splashing of the lake, questions were put to him; the desultory conversation stilled, and for an hour or two we listened, enthralled, to his incisive exposition, his sparks of humour, the clarity of his thinking, his patience in replying. My next, and closer, meeting with him was at Glastonbury staying in the mediaeval Pilgrim Hall converted into a hotel, for the initial production of Rutland Boughton's opera *The Immortal Hour*. At the end I had slipped quickly away and while waiting for my nightcap by the fire in the Pilgrim Hall the street door burst open and Shaw rushed in and over to the staircase. Half-way up he leaned over the bannisters, stage-whispered "Say you haven't seen me", and bolted for his bed-room. Next morning after breakfast he asked me to "come for a walk up the Tor". And up it, talking the whole way, his long legs strode while I, a quarter century younger, struggled breathlessly to keep up and reached the top incapable of contributing even a grunt.

In 1919, seeking support for the new type of theatre, I had written to Shaw and he agreed to see me at his flat, at the top of the old Adelphi with its fine view of the Thames, where, it is alleged, he and J. M. Barrie used to exchange rudenesses across the narrow side street. With Augustus John's 'Sleeping Philosopher' facing me by the fireplace I listened to his advice about money-raising. "You must never", he said, "look as if you need money. By fair means if possible, alternatively by foul, get yourself a new suit, shoes, linen, everything; *then* go and ask for donations and you'll get them." He himself never contributed a farthing and after the debacle of 1921 even exacted supplemental royalties but he spoke enthusiastically about the Everyman and people responded. At one time of crisis Lady Cunard telephoned saying rather plaintively "Bernard Shaw says I must give you £200. Why should I?" I gave reasons and made my plea. "But I can't spare £200" she said. I admitted that was awkward but "if G.B.S. said must . . . surely one must". "Well . . . I'll have to think" she said, and rang off. Some hours later Mr. George Dance telephoned, "Lady Cunard says I've got to give you £200. Why?" Again I gave good reasons and pressed my plea for the theatre. "But I've never even been to it" he said. I repeated my gambit—"unfortunate . . . but if Lady Cunard says 'must' . . . one must." "Oh very well," said he, and a little later his cheque arrived.

Shaw's rigid vegetarianism, catered for with special dull-looking dishes, was the subject of much amused comment, and later led to the classic story of Mrs. Patrick Campbell's outburst. "You wear Jaeger; you breathe Jaeger; you eat Jaeger; one day you'll eat an underdone steak and God help the women and children." At that Glastonbury time Shaw wore an old-fashioned Norfolk jacket and an equally antiquated style of knicker-bockers with 'cuffs' below the knee. Later he devised, as a compromise for functions or evening wear, a jacket and trousers of fluffy tweed dyed black, with an 'Anthony Eden' style of black felt hat. It was thus clothed that he rose one first night in response to the applause and calls for "Author", scurried to the side-exit, turning, called "In one moment the author won't be in the House" and disappeared into the street, leaving me to rescue Mrs. Shaw. Later I came to know both of them better. They began to come frequently to the Everyman to see new productions and spent the intervals in my office. Mrs. Shaw's encouragement was very comforting. Charles Macdona had been doing some of the plays with a touring company in the provinces and wanted to profit from the increasing success in London. Mrs. Shaw supported me in objecting and Macdona was told, "Charlotte wouldn't let me." On one occasion, passing through the foyer, Shaw heard someone speak of "MacDermott's audience" and immediately cracked "MacDermott hasn't got an audience—it's a congregation."

Fanny's First Play had not been performed since 1915. Its original production, by Shaw himself, with Lillah McCarthy had been in 1911. Surprisingly it had run for 622 performances; much the longest run of any Shaw play. We did not repeat the early success with it. Both production and performance were rough on the first night but the critics were kindly even though the play had many barbed shafts at well-known members of their craft. Several actually congratulated me on the revival, and wrote of the "excellent acting".

Arms and the Man had three productions before the war and one, with Robert Loraine, in 1919. Although not a great play it is very good theatre. It was very well received; the acting was called "superb" and "the best performance of this play I have seen". Milton Rosmer was specially praised that his "Bluntschli had a sense of humour and enjoyed the joke of reading the hotel inventory." The stock convertible-scenery was still in use and

perhaps because of a note in the programme about its economy
in use the settings received praise: "the setting and lighting was
a triumph of simplicity and beautiful effect" and "Rarely indeed
does one see so beautifully simple or so simply beautiful a scene
on the London stage as Raina's Bedroom" (*Illus.* 6).

Getting Married had not been performed since the original
Barker production in 1908. Pedantic critics were inclined to say it
was not a play because its dialogue continued unbroken for a
whole evening of "disquisitory talk". But what talk! "The wittiest
and most exhaustive discussion of marriage in literature." Its
brilliant argument was hugely enjoyed. "The audience at
Hampstead were truly (and very properly) thankful for what they
had received. . . ." "The talkers were as good as the talk."
"Superficially one would be inclined to say there is no opportunity
for real acting—as a matter of fact it calls for acting in its highest
form." Miss Gertrude Kingston, who had not been seen on stage
for some years, joined the Everyman to play Mrs. George and
stayed to play Mrs. Clandon in the coming continental visit.

Misalliance also had not been played since the original Frohman
repertory performances in 1910. It was not a success then, playing
for only 11 performances. I find a note that the critics then
"laughed heartily at the play but gave it bad notices and said they
had been bored". Fortunately it did better with us. Alfred Clark
as the thinly disguised Tycoon gave so rich, enjoyable and fruity
an interpretation that all the extravagances of the play became
natural. There was also "the loveliness of Miss Isabel Jeans who
dawned on us recently . . . and is certainly a capture for Hampstead". Again the excellence of the acting is noted and "the
performance must rank as one of the most creditable achievements
of Hampstead's dramatic centre".

There now occurred an event that added vastly to the repute
of the Everyman and gave us fresh confidence. The city of Zurich
was preparing an "Internationale Festspiele". This was one of the
earliest of the Festivals that are now an accepted part of artistic
and social life. France was to be represented by the company of
the Comédie Française; Germany by the Berlin State Theatre (in
Opera); and a delegation was in London to select an English
company. Dissatisfied with the plays they were seeing in the West
End, they were advised to make a journey to Hampstead and see
the current production at the Everyman. They came, unheralded,

to a performance of *Misalliance*. Next morning a Mr H. W. Draber telephoned and asked me to fix an appointment to see the delegates. At the meeting they seemed quite exhilarated and after exchange of questions and details of the proposal they formally invited me to take my company to represent Great Britain. Zurich would guarantee to pay all expenses including travel and hotels for the company. They particularly wanted plays by Shaw and Galsworthy as typical of the new English drama: *You Never Can Tell* (as we were playing it, with no changes) was stipulated and for Galsworthy *The Pigeon* which we had in preparation.

In the impressive and highly efficient State Theatre I felt extremely nervous and very humble in contrast to the French and German companies. Also very depressed indeed when we learned that for the first of our performances not half the seating was booked. Zurich had had English touring companies before and was taking no risks. But the first-night reception was boisterous and the press next day was more than enthusiastic. The leading paper, the *Neue Zürcher Zeitung* wrote: "we consider the Everyman performance of *You Never Can Tell* to be a particularly valuable item of this year's Festival." By afternoon that day every seat for our next performance was booked. Twenty years later the same paper, reviewing the visit of another English company, wrote that for real interpretation of English drama: "One must look back into Zurich theatre history of 1922. At that time Norman MacDermott's Everyman Theatre of London played in our summer festival Shaw's *You Never Can Tell* and Galsworthy's *The Pigeon*. They were two most impressive evenings. One learnt to recognise a superlatively fine technique showing the highest achievement of art."

In Zurich the artistes were greeted gaily in the streets and coffee-houses and were entertained in great lakeside mansions. After performances they went out on the lake in boats to revel in the moonlight, the impressive surrounding mountains, and to enjoy the chuckling water, followed by the Zürcher who gathered round to stare and to talk to the "englischen Schauspieler". It was alleged that on the Saturday night the company plotted to outstay the townfolk and that a launch had to be sent out to gather them in before dawn.

Our reputation had reached Geneva and there was an urgent invitation to give performances there. This we did at the Grand

Theatre on our way back to London, and the *Journal de Genève* wrote: "Enthusiasts who crowded the Grand Theatre were not disappointed. The English company gave them a perfectly finished performance of that admirable play by Bernard Shaw, *You Never Can Tell*." We could have stayed on for a further week at Geneva, Lausanne and Basle but the notice was too short for we had to return to London to complete the Shaw Season.

Meantime, to cover the absence of the main Company at Zurich I had arranged to present Ibsen's *Hedda Gabler* with Mrs. Patrick Campbell, who had played it years before, in the name part. Partly because I was engrossed in planning for the continental tour, and partly because I anticipated that difficulties with Hedda would have to be dealt with "managerially", I had asked that very finished actor J. H. Roberts, who had been playing with the company, to produce for me. And, forewarned, I was forearmed: Mrs. Pat was the only leading artiste with whom I had ever signed a specific written contract. No producer ever earned his fee more strenuously than Roberts. Every move had to be planned and replanned to suit Mrs. Pat. The actor for Lövborg was changed three times in the first fortnight of rehearsals: either Mrs. Pat would not accept them or they would not tolerate her rudeness which was continued *sotto voce* during performances. Everyone's nerves were breaking. An explosion was imminent when, late in the week before dress-rehearsals, with the opening announced for the following Tuesday, a trembling and tearful young assistant stage-manager came to me with the message: "Mrs. Patrick Campbell's compliments to Mr. MacDermott. She will be unable to open on Tuesday as she is going to Paris for the weekend about her dresses." My return message was: "Mr. MacDermott's compliments to Mrs. Patrick Campbell. It is impossible to postpone the first night. Tuesday has been booked with the West End Managers Association and there are other first-nights for the rest of the week." A few more tart exchanges, then I felt I had better go and face the music.

As I was using the stage to prepare the continental company, I had taken a near-by Hall for the *Hedda* rehearsals. Outside was a pleasant little courtyard with a lofty tree in the centre; opposite was a block of tenement buildings. The moment I was through the door of the Hall *the Voice* boomed, stripping me down to my antecedent and present vileness. I suggested the company was

being embarrassed and that we should go outside. We did: a
further salvo boomed and every tenement window became
occupied by a delighted spectator. The battleship of wrath became
overpowering. In a momentary pause I asked whether she had
read her contract? "What has THAT to do with it?" I pointed
out that even were the play a smash-hit her expenses were so high
that I should lose money, whereas if she did not appear on
Tuesday she would, under the forfeit clause, owe me £500. Her
eyes blazed; then with one of her sudden changes of mood she
said, "But how clever of you, I must kiss you!" And loudly she
did, to clapping and cheers from the impromptu audience.

The eventual performance was not satisfactory by our standards.
Mrs. Pat's personality dominated the stage and audience, of
course, but also swamped both play and the other artistes. It
provided, however, an opportunity for younger playgoers to see
a fabled actress in full gusto and for older West-Enders to savour
again flamboyance in full spate. But it was not Ibsen's *Hedda
Gabler* and I was reminded of Bernard Shaw's exasperated remark:
"You're not a professional actress; you are an inspired amateur".
There was a quaint repeat of the forgiving kiss on the first-night.
After curtain-fall the company were out of the theatre in a flash;
not even waiting to clean off their make-up, they vanished silently
into the night. Only professional courtesy left the girl A.S.M.
(Miss Henzie Raeburn, later a B.B.C. Programme Director) to
look after Mrs. Pat. In due time she summoned a taxi and as it
rolled down Fitzjohn's Avenue Mrs. Pat asked, "Well, my dear,
what did you think of me?" A wave of indignation overcame
the girl's nerves and she answered, "I think you are a vampire—
you suck the vitality out of everyone and then go on stage and
exploit us." "But," said Mrs. Pat, "How clever of you, I MUST
KISS YOU!" Another memory of that first-night is of the terrible
heat of the auditorium. The sun had blazed down on the thin roof
throughout a day of a heat record, the highest for thirty years.
To try to cool down the atmosphere we had bought, late in the
afternoon, three large zinc baths and had them filled with blocks
of ice. Before opening to the queue the stage-manager George
Carr and I, taking a last look round, were worried because there
was no sign of Mrs. Pat in her dressing-room. Then I noticed the
ice had completely melted. "Yes," said Carr, "obviously Mrs. Pat
is in." On return from Switzerland *Hedda Gabler* was transferred

to the Kingsway Theatre for a short run and the Continental part
of the company played *You Never Can Tell* for two weeks to complete its allocation in the Shaw Season, which then ended.

Then came one of the strange interludes in the Everyman story.
The Cambridge Marlowe Society had been giving performances
of Shakespeare's *Troilus and Cressida*, rarely performed at that
period. It had been enthusiastically reviewed by London critics
who urged that it ought to be shown in London. I offered the
Everyman stage for a week. It proved a costly gesture. Having
been fully reviewed at Cambridge the production was greeted at
the Everyman mainly by brief mention, while some paragraphists
referred to the Marlowe Society as amateurs. This was fatal and
audiences were very poor. It was also unjust: the cast included
many names that have since become famous in the theatre and
other spheres. The army of hefty young men left the dressing-
rooms, Green Room and corridors in such a condition of
greasepaint graffiti that the theatre had to be kept closed and
the whole of the following week was occupied in cleaning and
redecorating.

To accord with policy the theatre should then have closed for
the summer but the company, not wishing to be out of work for
three months, made a proposal to form themselves into a
'Commonwealth' to present plays until my re-opening for the
Autumn Season. Subject to holding a veto on plays to be
presented, and to maintenance of standards of production, I
agreed to this at a nominal rental. The arrangement worked well
and was loyally carried out. It also gave me a break much-needed
through illness. Their 'Commonwealth' Season opened in July
with a Triple Bill of one-act plays from our stock productions,
followed by *Candida*, then *Widowers' Houses*. This is not a good
play, but as the only previous performance of it had been by
Miss Horniman's Manchester Company in 1909 the Everyman
showing was welcomed as an unexpected opportunity of seeing
Shaw's first effort in drama. Seeking plays with small casts and
little scenery the 'Commonwealth' also revived Ibsen's *A Doll's
House*. They also put on *The New Sin* by Macdonald Hastings and
The Constant Lover by St. John Hankin with Leslie Banks in both
plays.

During this period the winding-up of the old Everyman
Theatre Ltd. reached the Courts and paragraphs in the press

gave the impression that the Everyman had collapsed. Rumour buzzed, and to counteract it a Notice was printed in all programmes for some weeks.

... recent notices in newspapers regarding the winding-up of "Everyman Theatre Ltd." have no reference whatever to the present Management of the theatre nor have they any effect on its continuance. Any connection of "Everyman Theatre Ltd." with the theatre was terminated in the middle of last year. Further notices of a similar nature will doubtless appear in newspapers during the course of the bankruptcy proceedings of the aforesaid company and all Friends of the Theatre are earnestly requested to make it clear wherever possible that the Theatre is in no danger of ceasing its work, as the policy and conduct of the Theatre since the change in Management has resulted in a steadily growing public interest and an increasingly satisfactory financial position.

The sunny summer, added to the social convention of not being in Town in July/August, was causing the company to have a very thin time and it would have been better to keep the theatre closed. In August, however, it proved possible to negotiate with John Drinkwater to present his *Mary Stuart* with himself producing. The long run of *Abraham Lincoln* at Hammersmith had given him wide repute and there was more preliminary publicity for *Mary Stuart* than for any other play presented at the Everyman. Drinkwater, as an original member of Barry Jackson's Birmingham Repertory Company, had experience of overcoming restricted working conditions and he secured an excellent performance. Miss Laura Cowie was added to the company to play the Queen, very beautiful and distinguished and giving a most appealing performance.

Mary Stuart opened in September. The press reception was very mixed, largely because critics had previous set-conceptions of Mary Stuart but knew little of Scotland's history. Both the romantics and the prejudiced were offended by the inherent sordidness of the background. Probably also they were annoyed by the author's rather condescending curtain speech. The play was, however, good theatre and Miss Cowie's portrayal one of those rare performances that playgoers eagerly respond to. Audiences began to increase. It was overdue to finish but the company pressed me to let it run beyond allotment while a West-End transfer was negotiated and so that they might recoup their earlier losses. Weeks drifted past but they did not secure any firm offer of transfer. Managements were probably influenced by some of the grudging notices but ought to have recognised that the beauty of Miss Cowie's performance, on top of the well-played intrigue and the convincing murder scenes, would have carried it to success with a wider audience.

The fortuitous long run of *Mary Stuart* had eased me through a period of illness and during convalescence I had time to study for one of my great ambitions. This was to produce a Shakespeare play in the way I thought it should be done—ignoring the then accepted 'versions', 'traditional-business', twisted characterisations. I chose *Twelfth Night*, the loveliest comedy in our literature; gay, tender, well-wrought and shapely, with masterly use of language. Certainly not, as then customary, merely a peg on which to hang a rag-bag of outworn slapstick. "Here we do the sword-business" would be anathema. No elaborate Palace Rooms should delay the progress of the action by scene-changes. Sir Toby, rousing the Night-Owle, should not turn the midnight scene into a boozy music-hall act. There should be no 'traditional business'; Shakespeare specified none; let him have his way for a change. Let us go quietly and humbly to our author and allow him to illumine the speaking of his words, and any action to arise directly from his lines. So should we 'show forth' the heart of the matter.

For years there had been much discussion and argument about appropriate settings for Elizabethan plays. There was grumbling at the over elaborate stagings of the Tree/Herkomer school, which entailed heavy cutting of text to keep within playing time; William Poel had used curtains and an almost bare stage; Norman Wilkinson had designed dignified simple but conventional stage settings for Granville Barker. With the established proscenium-style theatres, and audience demands for comfort and facilities, we could neither go back to a 'Wooden-O' nor bring de Witt's famous sketch indoors: some compromise had to be devised for the Everyman small stage. Long study and thought showed there were three fundamental essentials and that if these were provided the play would 'march' steadily and smoothly. These were simply: a main playing stage, an inner-room and a balcony over.

It has to be remembered that the Everyman was the first public theatre in London allowed to dispense with a Safety-Curtain and the fire-proof proscenium could not be removed or altered. A row of stalls was removed and the fore-stage extended; two pillars carried a 'masked' bridge for additional lighting. The back half of the stage was raised with two steps running the full width. Above the raised part a windowed balcony was built and under it a wide centre-opening with double folding doors. Open, these doors disclosed a small inner-stage where small rooms or entrance-ways could be quickly formed by placing tapestries or items of furniture. From the balcony a staircase led down to stage-level; and the corresponding 'block' opposite, with a grille, provided Malvolio's cell for the imprisonment. The whole set was painted ivory but the scenes changed colour completely by lighting (*Illus.* 7). All this had to be done on £30 which was the scene-allocation per production. The broken levels of the stage contributed to varied groupings. On the steps Sir Toby, Aguecheek and Feste sat and roistered, were 'shushed' by Maria, and taken to task by Malvolio from the balcony. Malvolio played the 'letter-scene' up and down the steps in full 'sunlight'; Sir Toby, Fabian and Aguecheek in the shade of the forestage using the pillars for hiding and stage-whispering, their cross-talk of indignation easily heard by the audience but, acceptably, not by Malvolio.

No cuts were made in the text: it was performed in full as written. It very sweetly sang its way along well within "the two hours traffic of our stage", broken only for the convenience of the audience. As to the playing we sought, intensely, for clarity of speaking; lovingly nursed beauty of phrase. Taking a cue from "it hath a dying fall" we allowed a pause, or a silence, to give the hearer time to savour a meaning. Was it a success? Let the critics tell: ". . . the Everyman production of *Twelfth Night* is the best Shakespearean revival I have ever seen in London." ". . . acted by people who realise that the heritage of our English tongue is a possession worth keeping . . . and . . . spoke their golden lines with a sensitiveness rarely heard on the English stage." ". . . the production aimed at, and achieved, a higher ideal than providing star-turns for intelligent actors . . . realising that there is something more important than Sebastian or Malvolio, which is *Twelfth Night* and something more important than *Twelfth Night* which is Shakespeare and Art." There was at any rate one member of the first-night audience who felt that a new chapter had been opened in the history of the English stage: thus wrote Francis Birrell in his review in the *New Statesman*, 30th December, 1922 (quoted on page 118).

Olivia.	Isabel Jeans (in her first golden wig) Bewitching . . . a sweet and captivating figure . . . perfectly beautiful, the freshest, young, Olivia we have ever seen.
Sir Toby.	The great virtue of the performance is the Sir Toby of Frank Cellier; one of the richest conceptions of the character I can remember; most ripe and unctuous in his humour.
Malvolio.	Herbert Waring is the best Malvolio I have ever seen.
Orsino.	Possibly the most gratifying of all was Mr. Baliol Holloway's Orsino.
Maria.	After a long succession of giggling Marias snatched from some musical comedy beauty-chorus; what a joy to see (Margaret Yarde) sweep on in broad Shakespearean humanity.
Feste.	Harold Scott . . . incomparable . . . his easiness of gesture and sympathetic voice made him the only Clown I have seen whom I should be glad to attach to my person.

Feste, of course, is in love with Olivia, his Mistress, though never daring to express it. At the close, as the characters *exeunt*, Feste, sitting by the arch, singing "for the rain, it raineth every day", stooped swiftly and kissed the hem of Olivia's gown as she passed. One learned what a variety and depth of feeling can be expressed in a "hey ho".

For contrast the paragraphists showed how they deluded themselves in their hunt after a startling caption. One wrote "an orgy of miscasting" and complained that "two fine actors (Ion Swinley and Baliol Holloway) were "thrown away on small parts", instead of being pleased that even small parts were played by fine actors. Another wrote of "the dim irritating light" while a colleague complained the stage was "so bright that it hurt his eyes"! Still another hated Sir Toby and Fabian "being brought forward" and wrote "one misses the box-hedge" (that ridiculous "prop" of painted canvas behind which they used to bob up and down plainly seen by Malvolio). Others wrote nothing of play or performance but concentrated on snide remarks about the new lighting installation.

I have written at some length about *Twelfth Night* because it seems to epitomise the Everyman story: the aims; the 'mania'; the difficulties; the achievement; the recognition, and often generous support, of the leading critics, as well as the niggling of the 'knocking' paragraphists.

This production might well have transferred for a West-End run but at that time of year theatres were filled with the customary Christmas light entertainment and any suggestion of changing to a Shakespeare play was dismissed as highbrow fantasy. Clearly such a cast as listed could not be kept together at Everyman salaries for more than a few weeks so it was impossible to wait on some sudden failure of seasonal entertainment and regretfully *Twelfth Night* was restricted to its allotted three weeks.

For our customary Children's Matinées in the Christmas period we had prepared a stage full of animals and of musical fantasy based on the *Uncle Remus Stories* by Mabel Dearmer, with music by Martin Shaw who supervised the musical side. The production was by Harold V. Neilson with many additions, mainly children, to form a large cast including Hayden Coffin in the singing part and Nadine March for Brer Rabbit. Dodie Smith was also in the company at this time. The attractive costumes were designed by Miss Peggy Fremantle. *Brer Rabbit* was an unqualified success and the press notices were only a gratifying addition to the delighted glee of the packed child audiences.

Scene IV: 1923

For policy in the new year it was important to consider not only avoidance of the one-man label but also the encouragement of new writers. A number of new plays by unknown authors were awaiting production: *Medium* by Leopold Thoma, *At Mrs. Beam's* by C. K. Munro and *T'Marsdens* by J. R. Gregson, which would alternate with Shaw plays.

Medium was by a famous Viennese psychiatrist, Leopold Thoma, and had been translated from the German by George Merritt who had played in German theatres and was now a permanent member of the company. It was given a good cast and performance and in the press had lengthy analytical notices of its importance in criminal psychology. Although it interested the critics it had very poor audiences: in fact in the second week the receipts touched the record lowest ever of £4 10s. for the whole week, and it was hastily withdrawn.

Included in the same programme was a charming one-act French play *A Perfect Day*, translated by Mrs. Alfred Sutro. I had seen a performance of the original at Copeau's Vieux Colombier in Paris with Louis Jouvet in the cast and I frankly shaped our performance on that. It is a pity that this play was linked with one that did not attract audiences. The failure of *Medium* sent me hastily to the safety of Shaw but, wishing to hold his more important plays for Spring and a Shaw Season, I turned to *The Philanderer*, his second play, which had not been performed since the first production in public in 1907. Though not Shaw at his best it created considerable interest for its "wit, spontaneous and caustic". Milton Rosmer played Charteris and produced it. Julia Craven was played by Hilda Moore.

The next play *At Mrs. Beam's* proved of special significance in the Everyman story. It was by an unknown writer, a civil servant, C. K. Munro. It had been given a single performance on a Sunday by the Stage Society which I had missed. I asked for a script and was excited to find a play I judged of Everyman standard but also, I felt certain, one which would please a wider public. It was an extravagant comedy set in a Bloomsbury boarding house with a curious collection of guests. It had amusing situations, surprise, and lines that brought gusts of spontaneous laughter such as are rarely heard. Miss Jean Cadell's performance as the frustrated Miss Shoe is still referred to, forty years later, as "a classic of acting". The very dear and beautiful Hilda Moore as a 'nice' adventuress in a love scene with Bill Monk as a desperately shy and awkward youth was rich and unforgettable.

At Mrs. Beam's was an immediate smash hit and offers for transfer came from three managements. I was in a position to be choosy but also had the difficulty to overcome that Franklin Dyall, in the leading part, was under a film contract and due to leave the company. One of the offers, however, came from Mr. Dennis Eadie at the Royalty Theatre, who wished to play the part of Mr. Dermott himself, and I gladly completed a contract to open in six weeks time when his current play would end.

I had meantime received another official continental invitation. This time to take the company to Holland in *The Pigeon*. I now offered *At Mrs. Beam's* as an alternative. The Dutch representatives came to see it and readily accepted the change. We could just fit in the ten days playing at The Hague, Amsterdam, Haarlem, and Rotterdam, and be back in time to settle in at the Royalty on the agreed date. This time I had chosen not a Guarantee but a percentage of profits from which, if the tour was successful, a profit might result. It was, of course, long before there was any British Council or Arts Council financial support for theatre. I thought, however, we were entitled to some form of official support and I sought an interview at the Foreign Office. An appointment was made, and very courteous they were, but there the interest stopped: they would not even agree to forego the 5s. fee on each passport for the company. Our Minister at The Hague must, however, have been advised for, rather grudgingly, he and a party attended the first night. They became so enthusiastic that he took a box at Amsterdam for the last night there.

At the end of the run of *At Mrs. Beam's* the awkward young man asked whether he might stay on in the company but, not seeing any immediate parts for him, I advised him to go back to the Old Vic for another year. He went to see Miss Baylis and she agreed to his return. He then said that following his West-End success he thought he ought to have a better salary than before; he would like to have five pounds a week instead of three. Then followed a delightful little scene:

Miss B. Do you believe in God?
Monk. Er . . . Yes.
Miss B. Then you believe in Prayer.
Monk. Well. . . . Yes!
Miss B. Then kneel down. This is my chair. You have that one *Short pause.* I've got a young man with me who wants to be taken into my company but he says he wants Five Pounds a week.
After a longer pause Miss B got briskly to her feet.
God says Four.
And four pounds it had to be.

To complete the arrangements for the Royalty Theatre and for collection of our scenery on its return at London Docks I travelled back in advance of the company. *At Mrs. Beam's* ran at the Royalty until the end of the year and my share of the profits was the first earned endowment of the Everyman Theatre, the weekly share-cheque being paid straight into the theatre account. The visit to Holland combined with the 'settling-in' at the Royalty entailed some adjustment of plans, and to give a time margin a 'Let' of the theatre (under the 'By Arrangement' formula) was accepted from Mr. Gordon Bailey to present *The Alternative* by Lucy Wilson and Adrian Alington. It had little success, was withdrawn, and the theatre again stood empty.

The third experimental new play was put on between two forthcoming Shaw productions. It was *T'Marsdens* by J. R. Gregson, a Yorkshire writer. The main part of the company being at the Royalty in *At Mrs. Beam's*, additions were necessary to fill the gaps. This allowed recruitment of three well-known character actors most suitable for the type of part in the play: Charles Groves, Edward Rigby, Frank Pettingell. Good though it was, and with such skilled comedians as added attraction, London showed it could not care less how Yorkshire lived.

The main plays I had chosen for this third Shaw Season were *The Doctor's Dilemma* and *Major Barbara*; two which give me greatest satisfaction. I could give them near-perfect casts; and I

opposite: Illus. 10 *The Mask and the Face.* 1924
(See page 62)

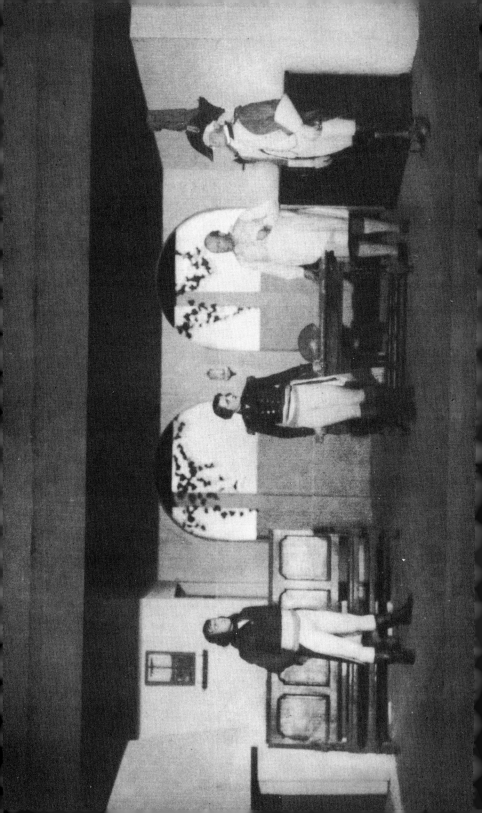

wanted to test myself again as producer. I had arranged with Claude Rains to join the company for a series of plays and his first part was Louis Dubedat in the *Dilemma*. Cathleen Nesbitt had just returned to London after absence in America and I was able to cast her for Jennifer. I wanted to present the play without the 'afterthought' in a Bond Street Picture Gallery. I never liked the scene; it is not integral to the play and seems tacked on as though Shaw had suddenly had one of his self-conscious turns and felt ashamed of the genuine feeling displayed in the earlier acts. Moreover it makes the performance too long and necessitates an additional, and difficult, set. With a long scene-change at the worst time in the evening there is a damaging hiatus and it is no help to say "Well . . . three weeks have passed since the funeral". That is not the feeling of the audience and they simply do not believe in the cold switch in Jennifer. But Shaw was adamant and it had to be played in full or not at all.

Cathleen Nesbitt as Jennifer was excellent: Rains gave a superb performance and the death-scene was quite unforgettable. The audience acclaim at the curtain convinced me that the play could have been transferred to the West End for a long run. One of my most satisfying memories is of the rise of the curtain on the group of doctors round the oval dinner-table on a terrace of the Hotel at Richmond; comfortably replete, lit only by the glow from an unseen table-centre bowl; a thread of cigar-smoke spiralling against the blue sky. The picture was held for some moments before a word spoken and the peaceful relaxation of the group made an appropriate lead-in to the Act. It was received with many an appreciative comment. Except from the artistes: economy ruled there must be only one cigar per performance and there was nightly rivalry as to who should get it, the others had to be content with cigarettes and cold-tea in their brandy balloons.

The *Major Barbara* cast was as near perfect as one could wish. Dorothy Massingham again as Barbara, quite perfect; the clean dry edge of Aylmer's Cusins; the sardonic weight of Jeayes's Undershaft, and Ethel Coleridge in her original part setting the key for the Salvation Army shelter-yard. With such a play and such a cast what more could any producer, or any audience, ask. And the author? He had not come to rehearsals but came to performances. One of my happiest memories is of him chortling with delight. He noted the increasing strength and quality of the

opposite: Illus. 11 *The Man of Destiny.* 1924.
Claude Rains and Jeanne de Casalis
(See page 64)   *Photograph by* Bertram Park

company and the performances they were giving, and spoke specially of Felix Aylmer "the best Cusins I have ever had"; of Dorothy Massingham as "exactly Barbara"; seemed deeply impressed by Rains's Dubedat; and even wrote in my copy of the play "The best performance this play has had".

My last production before summer closing was a special performance on a Sunday for the 'Friends of the Everyman'. The play was *Beyond Human Power* by Bjornsterne Bjornsen, a Norwegian dramatist considered by many to be at least the equal of Ibsen, but then, and even now, practically unknown in England. In this Irene Rooke gave a performance of such beauty and so deeply moving that the audience remained still and silent after the curtain fell—the greatest accolade an artiste can win.

Casts like these were, by West-End salary scales, prohibitive but I was offering to artistes parts of such interest and importance that they were not only ready but eager to come to the Everyman at its modest salary rates which were now based on a minimum ranging from five pounds to fifteen pounds per week with, in special cases, a percentage of House-Receipts after Costs. Even so, the weekly salary list was too high to be carried by Everyman takings even when the audience was running to an average of 75 to 80 per cent capacity. This surplus of costs over receipts was now being met by the profits from the West-End transfers and thus the Everyman was, in fact, an 'endowed' theatre.

Again the company proposed a 'Commonwealth' for the summer instead of closing the theatre and the same arrangement as in 1922 was agreed. They commenced as before with repeats from the repertoire: *Candida, Fanny's First Play, Mary Stuart,* and added Chesterton's *Magic* which proved very popular. They then presented that strange play *Outward Bound* by Sutton Vane, in which the passengers in the Smokeroom of a cruise liner gradually realise that they are all dead and are crossing the river Styx. Stanley Lathbury as the Smokeroom Steward/Charon gave an eerie and very telling performance that established the peculiar 'atmosphere'. The play was an immediate success and was transferred quickly to the West End for a run. Later it had several revivals, became popular with amateur societies and continued to be performed for many years afterwards. The quick transfer to the West End caused a gap which was filled by a 'By Arrangement' let to Milton Rosmer who produced and presented two comedies for two weeks each. *Ancient Lights* by Edward Percy and *What the Public Wants* by Arnold Bennett. Both plays had strong casts of regular Everyman players.

When I resumed presentations in the Autumn, two new plays by new authors were waiting production. The first was *The Second Round* by Halcott Glover. It was a sound play and worth giving a trial, but neither critics nor public liked it and it had to be withdrawn after nine performances. Another attempt to launch a new dramatist failed. Pending the Christmas production the theatre was let for a comedy by May Hazell Marshall, again with a cast of Everyman artistes, produced by Milton Rosmer. This also was withdrawn and the theatre closed. A performance to establish copyright of the play *The Mask and the Face* which was to be my first spring 1924 production was given during the 'closed' period.

For the Christmas Season a special production was again planned, in association with a Group named Alpha Productions, largely at the instance of Harold Scott who produced it. This was Isaac Bickerstaffe's 18th-century Comic Operetta *Love in a Village* with music by Dr. Arne. The four-piece orchestra was conducted by Julian Herbage; costumes were designed by the artist Rupert Lee; the charming French diseuse Raymonde Collignon sang Rosetta. There was some hope that the public would respond as they had to *The Beggar's Opera* at Hammersmith but it was not sufficiently well reviewed.

Before leaving the year 1923 some ancillary activities, efforts to add additional interests for the audience and efforts to supplement income should be noted. Among the first, Exhibitions in the small foyer of paintings, drawings, etc. were regularly mounted. Two canvases lent by Mr. J. Holroyd-Reece were the first Van Gogh and Gauguin paintings to be shown publicly in London. Hampstead artists were given monthly shows, including a collection of Edmond Kapp's portrait cartoons; Jean Inglis portraits; the original costume designs by John Garside and Randolph Schwabe, and Austrian and Hungarian posters.

Taking advantage of the extremely favourable rate of foreign exchange I bought in Munich 'peasant' furniture and wrought-iron work, table-glass, embroidered and hand-printed fabrics and, in Vienna, fine furs, exquisite silks and wrought metal-ware by famous artists. These, exhibited in the theatre and sold at seeming throw-away prices, not only spread artistic repute but made many hundreds of pounds for our exchequer.

For Lady Fortescue, who was launching into *haute couture* while Sir John wrote the official History of the British Army, we gave one dress-show in the theatre and, taking lighting apparatus, lit another evening display in the garden of the Admiral's House in Hampstead, where they lived. Scenery and lighting for amateur companies was undertaken including an installation at the Citizen House Theatre, Bath. A notice was printed in all programmes:

THE EVERYMAN STUDIOS

Decorations, Furnishings, Clothes, Ladies Gowns, Evening Wraps, Fancy Dress Costumes, Furniture, Decoration Schemes, Lampshade and lighting effects undertaken.

A number of orders were received and eventually a major commission that led to a significant donation to the theatre.

One evening at the end of the performance three people in the audience asked to see me. They were a Lancashire cotton merchant, Mr. F. E. Lowry, his wife and daughter. About to leave for America, where he would buy modern machinery for his mills, they had come to London to set themselves up in clothes for the tour but had been unable to get promise of delivery in limited time nor to find suitable things 'off the peg': they wanted quality materials and fine silks. Could we undertake the commission and guarantee delivery before sailing in just over a week? We had a most able wardrobe mistress, and by working all day and several nights and calling in assistants from our part-time list the order was completed. Dresses, linen costumes, summer coats proved to be a remarkable success throughout their tour of the U.S.A. and Canada and on return they called to thank us. Mr. Lowry later expressed it in the form of a four-figure cheque to enable me to buy in Germany a complete new Phoebus lighting installation for the Everyman. In after years the Lowrys became some of the most beneficent supporters of experimental plays. Another such supporter was Mr. Alfred Kohnstamm of Hampstead who many times responded with a substantial cheque when some play flopped and the takings would not meet salaries and wages.

Scene V: 1924

The repute of the theatre was now such that there were continuous applications by *ad hoc* managements or producing groups for short tenancies to try out new plays. In addition numerous plays were offered with down payments towards the cost of production. Such arrangements as were accepted were dissociated from my productions by special wording on posters and programmes but this did not entirely save the management of the theatre from criticism and attack.

In the first half of 1924 too many of these were agreed in the effort to keep losses from sinking the ship: *The Morals of Vanda, Love in a Village, The Painted Lady, Young Imeson, Monica, In and Out, The Tropic Line,* and *Her Daughter* which was thankfully announced as "The last of the productions under special contracts". Most of them were described by the authors as farcical-comedies and it was a grave disappointment that the effort and money provided to encourage new playwrights brought no better results.

Better policy might have been to close the theatre for a spell until a number of good plays had been found, but that would have entailed disbanding the company and the loss of the team-work that was so important a factor in keeping up our standards. Although the experiment was well-intended it was a blunder, costly in both money and repute and also in support by the critics who, naturally, grew impatient. Here is one example of the dilemma: passing through the foyer on one such first night I saw a group of four of the leading critics of London. One of them, E. A. Baughan, then the doyen of theatre critics, held out to me his programme with his thumb emphasising the 'By Arrangement' Note. "Does this mean what I think it means?" he said. "Yes," I replied. "How much?" "Several Hundreds." "Oh! . . . Well! We'll let you off this time—but don't do it on us again."

On the other hand, it must be remembered that an experimental production could bring another winner like *At Mrs. Beam's* and save the whole situation. And so it proved. I had one play contracted for presenting in which I had the greatest confidence. This was an English version, made by C. B. Fernald, of *La Maschera e il Volto* by Luigi Chiarelli. I had had it in preparation for some time but plans were be-devilled by three different writers claiming they held the English performing rights. There had been a sample of this danger over *The Bonds of Interest* and I was chary. The trouble arose because during the war period American authors had secured the rights of translation of many important continental plays. In the case of *The Mask and the Face* the matter was further complicated by Fernald having made a number of alterations in shaping his brilliant version; modifying some passages and situations in the original that certainly would not have recommended the script to the Lord Chamberlain.

This involved the author Chiarelli, who seemed evasive, and in an exchange of letters with him I had to be quite definite that I would present Fernald's version or none at all. For three weeks in January I had to keep the theatre closed while Fernald fought the legal position and Court proceedings were staved off. Eventually, however, the way was clear and the curtain opened on the 5th February to an immediate and exciting success.

This was one of the high-spots of Everyman productions. Even the delay contributed by allowing ample time for rehearsal and detail. The casting was precisely right and the whole company were imbued with Everymania. The setting was one of the most successful and there were no waits or lighting troubles. The laughter was delighted and continuous even through long passages without a word spoken when the movement and business added inventively to the dialogue. Athene Seyler as the supposedly unfaithful wife, supposedly drowned in Lake Como by her supposedly indignant husband, prinking in to her own funeral service is a moment never to be forgotten by those who saw it. Another husband's whisper to his wife "The dye is coming off on your neck" is funnier because it was so natural. Frank Cellier's poker-faced playing of the Count Mario's self-righteous dumbness was a triumph of comedy acting (*Illus.* 10).

There were several offers for immediate transfer but again I could be choosy and wait for the best theatre for comedy, the

Criterion, meantime keeping it on at Hampstead for six weeks, until it was duly transferred and ran for nearly a year. The dresses were designed by Miss Dorothy Warren who was acting in the play, and whose help in several ways I remember very gratefully. Among other contributions she brought Lady Diana Manners to the penultimate dress rehearsal and that I am sure started the bush telegraph that brought a 'Rolls and Mink' full-house on the first night.

The Everyman now had its second endowment through the profits from the Criterion: a substantial weekly sum, month after month. It was exasperating that so much of it went in meeting the losses from uncharacteristic plays. Moreover a further financial burden had to be faced. The rent of the Everyman which had been ten pounds a week when I took over had now been increased to thirty pounds a week. Each success in the West End was followed by a demand for an increase of ten pounds, backed by a threat of two weeks Notice to terminate the tenancy. Recovery of repute and of goodwill must needs be quick and I reverted to the slogan "When in doubt—play Shaw". I announced: *The Man of Destiny, Getting Married, The Devil's Disciple, Misalliance,* and *Androcles and the Lion.* The Shaw Plays would not be restricted to three-week runs but would vary with the audience interest. There was to be no summer 'Commonwealth'. These would be interspersed with two new plays that I had bought: *Low Tide* by Ernest George and a play by the Hungarian author Ladislas Fodor which I had seen in performance in Budapest and was now translating. Possibly two short 'Lets' might be taken to space the Shaw plays for rehearsal time.

Again with part of the company in the West End there were gaps to fill in casting and fortunately some admirable additions to the company became possible. Claude Rains was now free to rejoin the company permanently for the series of parts I had proposed to him. Others were Edith Evans, Jeanne de Casalis and Olive Sloane.

The first play of this new Shaw series was *The Man of Destiny.* It was practically unknown and had not been performed since the Vedrenne–Barker Season in 1907, and then only for eight matinées. Claude Rains' Napoleon was "a masterpiece. He wears not merely Napoleon's uniform but his air of vital significance as well." Jeanne de Casalis, who had been playing at Jacques

Hebertot's Théâtre de Champs Elysées and had written asking to be included in the Everyman Company, was "The strange Lady". She gave a delightful, gay and subtle performance and carried off the uniform most gallantly. One critic made the astonishing prophecy: "Claude Rains was very amusing and his facial expression so amazing that he might well enter the 'Film-world' with the dictum 'my face is my fortune'—and it would be. What a screen comedian lives before us in him" (*Illus.* 11).

The Man of Destiny is a short play and has to be accompanied by a one-act morsel. Shaw proposed *Augustus does his Bit*. After seeing it he agreed to it being replaced by *How he lied to her Husband*. We treated this as sheer slapstick farce with Felix Aylmer as the over-dignified husband and Harold Scott as the intense lover. Shaw again had not been at rehearsals but came to a performance when he rocked with laughter and called out "It's an outrage! but I never laughed so much in my life".

The next was *Getting Married* and Edith Evans was an ideal Mrs. George. "Other actresses have played the part but she easily eclipses them all." The reviews were all that one could wish and even more was the audience response so that the production was allowed to run for five weeks.

The first break for a new play experiment was made here with *Low Tide* by Ernest George. He had had a widely varied career from East-End newsboy, waiter, office clerk, until, with his wife whom he met in a theatre-gallery queue, he started a bookshop. George Merritt, then acting in *The Mask and the Face*, called seeking a Dunsany volume, became a regular customer and encouraged George to write a play of the dock life he knew so intimately. Ultimately Merritt brought the play to me and the *Evening News* quotes me as saying the author is "wonderfully true in his delineation of the people he writes about and he shows in his play a marvellous sense of the theatre". This romantic story of authorship produced columns of pre-publicity. The play got lengthy favourable notices; the author was welcomed as revealing great possibilities as a new playwright, the "intensity and truth of his dialogue" were compared to the work of Eugene O'Neill. The cast received unlimited praise, particularly Rains for his portrayal of the sheer physical brutality of the bully "not an inch that was not acting, from the muscles of his neck to the jut of his thigh". Of Ethel Coleridge: "given a chance she too seldom gets took it with both hands—one forgot it was acting and only felt that here was the real thing". Similarly for the rest of the cast. Of Olive Sloane, extremely beautiful in a part very different to those for which she was known: "tonight had a part that demanded emotion and she carried it off with real success". "The Author must consider himself fortunate to have such a cast for his first play." "Everyone who is interested in play writing and in acting should go to the Everyman to see this very vivid picture" (*Illus.* 12).

There was the feel of an important occasion. Transfer to the West End for a run was prophesied by a number of critics. But audiences did not come in sufficient numbers. Why? Partly the old indifference to the way low life is lived, emphasised in this case by one incident in the play. In front of the cringing husband the bully strikes the girl a vicious blow. This was most carefully rehearsed and superbly played; with doubled fist Rains apparently struck Olive Sloane full in the face and, with a miracle of technique, she keeled right over backwards flat on the stage (*Illus.* 13). One could hear the horrified gasp of the audience. It is a pleasing thought that they were really shocked. My shock came through the Box Office, and the play had to be taken off after five performances. In two papers a paragraphist, probably the same one, complained bitterly about "realism carried too far" because in his fourth-row stall "there was an intolerable odour from a real paraffin lamp on the table throwing out its fumes to the audience and probably inconveniencing the performers". The lamp was a real paraffin lamp but converted to electric by battery: the Fire Inspectors would never have allowed us to light a candle, let alone paraffin on the stage.

So "Back to Shaw" as one paper headlined it; and another, "East, West, Shaw's best". Fortunately there was still a steady demand at the box office for *The Man of Destiny* and this was restored to the Bill, so soon as *How he lied to her Husband* could be set and polished. A critic wrote "If it is always played with the cleverness of last night it ought to provide laughter for another twenty years". The next Shaw play *The Devil's Disciple*, had not been performed since the Vedrenne–Barker Season in 1907. Even some of the critics noted they had neither seen nor read it. It came as a complete surprise to playgoers. Although called a melodrama it was discovered to be a "feast of wit", created delighted interest, and was described (with *Blanco Posnet*) as "ancestor of *St. Joan*". The cast and performance got the praise that was now almost standard recognition of the ability of the company and also of Rains' outstanding quality. His Dudgeon was praised as "far more robust in his devil-may-careness" than the original Murray Carson, Granville Barker, or Sir Johnston Forbes-Robertson. More than one critic called for its transfer to the West End: "The sooner it comes the better." "A rare intellectual treat."

Shaw's *Mrs. Warren's Profession* had been banned from public performance since it was written in 1893/4. I had submitted it to the Lord Chamberlain several times for licence. Three times it had been refused but unexpectedly I now heard on my fourth application that a licence would be granted. The announcement to the press that it would be the next production at the Everyman naturally received extensive publicity. But a peculiar complication arose, and led to my only serious disagreement with Shaw. Following on the success of the Everyman revivals of the Shaw Plays, the Charles Macdona Company was playing some of them in the provinces, recently had given some performances in Paris, and was about to do a short season at the Regent Theatre at King's Cross. I had an understanding, or working arrangement, with Shaw that he would not grant London performing rights to Macdona of any of the plays that he had agreed to my presenting. Macdona now announced that he would include *Mrs. Warren* at the Regent. I protested to Shaw at this invasion of my territory. Shaw quibbled that the Regent was not a West-End theatre but provincial. Macdona announced a postponement until October; and later a further postponement "until the spring—with an all-star cast". I did not intend to enter a bickering conflict over the play and stopped preparations. The play was not, in fact, seen in the West End until 1926 when it was presented by Macdona and Arthur Bourchier, with the latter playing the lead. By that time I was finally out of the theatre world for the next ten years.

Instead of *Mrs. Warren* there followed a hilarious revival of *Misalliance* in which Shaw's tendency to slide into slapstick farce was given full rein. Dorothy Green joined the company to play Lina Szczepanowska and Alfred Clarke to play Tarleton the tycoon of the period. The vocal contrast in performances which Shaw, rightly, considered most important was given full range between Rains's rich volume, Aylmer's crisp clean dryness, Margaret Yarde's fruity richness, Ivor Barnard's terrified twitter; and it was reviewed as "one of the wittiest of Shaw's Comedies". Even that stern critic Desmond MacCarthy wrote: "The play is not one of Shaw's masterpieces but it exhibits his extraordinary power of making discussions so amusing that on stage it throws most comedies of situation in the shade as entertainment." In colloquial terms it "went like a riot" and press notices grew even warmer.

Then followed a 'Let' for *Clogs to Clogs* by John Walton. It had a good cast and was "admirably performed" but had the same fate as other low-life plays; summed up by the *Daily Telegraph*: "The humour . . . is of the eye rather than the ear. . . . This is precisely the difference between London and Lancashire. Bring the play to Manchester and this judgment would be reversed."

The Shaw series was now interrupted for the last experimental play of this year. As it proved to be a major success, the story of its selection may be worth telling as a notable instance of the 'chancy' character of play discovery. A mound of unread scripts had accumulated and to reduce it I had given batches of half-dozens to Stage-Manager; Business-Manager; and a 'Friend of the Everyman' who was very knowledgeable about the continental theatre. They were to be returned to me with some brief particulars and marked "To be read", or "N.B.G.", or the like. During the run of *Misalliance* I went for a short weekend to a quiet country hotel to concentrate on solving a difficulty in the version I was making of the play by Ladislas Fodor which I had bought in Budapest. At the last moment before leaving I put one of the returned batches of plays in my bag. The translation difficulty was solved during Saturday but the rain put even a walk out of the question. I turned to the scripts. Four of these were marked "To be read"; they provided a lengthy boredom. Searching the residents' lounge for something to read I found only an old *Punch* and an even older railway A.B.C. On Sunday evening when I went down to supper all the reading left to me was two scripts marked "N.B.G." At midnight I was reading both for the second time: one was *Hay Fever* and the other was *The Vortex*.

On Monday morning by catching the "milk train" I was back in the theatre by nine o'clock and seeking Noël Coward by telephone. A slight play by him had been done at the Savoy theatre with himself and Miss Kate Cutler in the leading parts but it had little success. Accordingly, with their customary blindness, West-End Managers would not risk any other play by the same author: these two scripts had been the rounds of every Manager and Agent and had been universally declined. Miss Cutler, who believed in Coward's ability and warmly encouraged him, had brought the plays to me. Coward was contacted and came to see me on the Tuesday. I told him I would put on both plays, *The Vortex* first. Coward wanted *Hay Fever* first but although it was the better play I insisted on *The Vortex* which I considered a sure-fire success and in view of his two previous failures it seemed right to hit hard with his third play.

Coward himself was the Producer and though there were a few Everyman artistes in the cast the artistes were mostly friends of his. The settings and the ladies' dresses were designed by his colleague Mrs. Gladys Calthrop, but the Everyman allocation would not stretch to the standard he wanted and Mr. Michael Arlen lent him a sum to cover the costs. Rehearsals commenced with Miss Kate Cutler in the leading part. After some days she came to me and regretfully but very firmly resigned the part saying that she could not continue to bear with Coward's studied rudeness in front of the company. I asked her to return to rehearsal and I went quietly to my Director's seat. I could not but agree that it was impossible for her to continue. Afterwards I told Coward that Miss Cutler had resigned and had left the theatre. His reply came simply "Lilian Braithwaite will be rehearsing to-morrow". *The Vortex* was well advanced in rehearsal when I received a message that Lord Cromer would like to see me about it and I duly went to St. James's. He went through a tabbed copy pointing out one or two minor word-cuts and then referred to a throw-away line about two women friends who had gone to Venice together. He agreed that he could not see what was wrong with it and suggested that the Reader should be consulted. The explanation was that it implied they were Lesbians and that could not be allowed on the stage. I said that the author's contract stipulated there should be no change of word without his consent and I must consult Coward. Back at the theatre I told Coward, who rocked with amusement, saying "If only I had thought of that myself". I arranged for him to see Lord Cromer and he returned saying "No bother at all".

The contract for the two Coward plays were waiting signature. As there was no sign of this before the last week of rehearsals I asked him for it; and finally at dress-rehearsal weekend told him I would not send up the curtain on Tuesday unless I had his signed copy by then. On the Monday afternoon a signed contract reached me for *The Vortex* only.

The Vortex was transferred to the Royalty Theatre in December. Apart from the business side of the transfer I was excluded from playing any part in the celebration of its success. Although, at the time and afterwards, there was no word of appreciation either written or spoken, I like now to reflect that it was my theatre, my money, my judgment, that gave him that first chance. No contract for *Hay Fever* ever came and that play was shortly contracted to another Manager and later presented at the Ambassadors Theatre.

The success story of *The Vortex* is too well known to need repeating, but its transfer made impracticable the usual special matinées of a play for children at Christmas. For the evening performances Shaw's *The Philanderer* was included to complete the announced series. It had been presented in the 1923 Season and withdrawn from repertoire but with a stronger cast, including Claude Rains, Felix Aylmer and Dorothy Massingham, again produced by Milton Rosmer, the press notices confirmed: "A first-class performance . . . the Company being one which many a West-End theatre would be glad to possess." It ran through the Christmas Season and into January.

Scene VI: 1925

With the 1924 record of *The Mask and the Face* at the Criterion, *The Vortex* at the Royalty, *The Philanderer* bringing good audiences to the Everyman, and another sure-fire winner ready for rehearsal, I felt not too far from the top of the theatre world. The rent had gone up again, this time by an added percentage of receipts, but I had gone forward confidently, or over-optimistically, with plans for the ensuing year.

In January my version of Ladislas Fodor's play which he has described as a "satire on politics and a comedy of married life" was presented under the title of *Home Affairs*. A young politician with a popular policy of "Cradle, Hearth, and Home" finds himself, late in the evening of his wedding-day, elected as a Minister and hurries away from his waiting wife to attend his new duties. Parts of it 'in the French manner' would be too much for London and I had to make, not a translation, but a version. Even so, I had no trouble with the Lord Chamberlain although, as one critic wrote, "it provoked a woman to giggle delightedly, 'I don't know how Norman MacDermott dared' ". Others wrote that: "it had not, as is usual, suffered by its channel crossing"; "as amusing and shameless a piece of satire as has graced the chaste boards of a London theatre for a long time past". Other critics named the distinguished audience, . . . "their Sables". . . . "such ropes of pearls". . . . "diamond earrings hanging to her shoulders". . . . "lovely old lace shawl"; and "Lady Cunard springing to her feet and calling 'Brilliant, Brilliant' ".

The notices were almost the best that any Everyman production had: several critics prophesied it would be transferred quickly to the West End. Enquiries for transfer started within days. Three different theatres were on offer. But each Management wanted to change the player of the leading part from Claude Rains to some matinée idol. When I refused and asked for an explanation they said 75 per cent of all audiences were women;

Rains was too "short and stocky" and women would not see a lover in him! To us, who knew Rains had only to lift that wicked quizzing eyebrow for every woman present to give an ecstatic sigh, this was at first a joke; then infuriating stupidity. Finally I refused two firm offers in which the change was made a condition. Apart from any reason other, loyalty to Rains who had given so many distinguished performances and given also so generously of spirit left no other decision. His subsequent film career proves how imperceptive conventional theatre managers can be.

C. B. Fernald, the translator of *The Mask and the Face*, had made a play with Mrs. Clement Scott and urged me to let him present it himself. I could not be enthusiastic about the play but agreed as a sort of *quid pro quo* for *The Mask*. *Yvelle*, the new play, was seriously reviewed by the critics but it did not seem to have the sparkle and wit expected from its author and it lasted only a few performances.

The next play *It happened in Ardoran* had been done by the Stage Society as one of their Sunday productions, and I was asked to give place for it, 'By Arrangement'. It was a pleasant Scottish play but thin: it also was withdrawn after a few performances. These two plays should have occupied the stage for six weeks but between them gave only eighteen performances and the theatre remained closed for the remainder of the time of these 'Lets'.

The next major experimental production was *The Painted Swan* by (Princess) Elizabeth Bibesco. I think it an interesting and witty play and still cannot understand the almost scathing reception by some critics. It was given what, by now, was called the full Everyman treatment: an "overwhelmingly good cast", including Edith Evans, looking superbly beautiful as she can, Felix Aylmer, Frank Cellier, Alan Jeayes, and Elissa Landi in her first appearance on any stage, so lovely that her quick succession to stardom followed as no surprise. There were also two of the best sets (*Illus.* 14 *and* 15), furniture from a famous antique dealer, ample rehearsal, and a really distinguished and friendly audience, including the author's father, the late Prime Minister, who responded enthusiastically. Described by some as downright good drama the "sparkling epigram and paradox" was apparently too much for the run of critics. I kept it on for the full three weeks, expecting that the authoress' rendering of the renowned Asquith

wit, one of Edith Evans's most brilliant and likeable performances, and the notices of "a distinguished production of a
characteristic West-End Play" would make it next night's
dinner-talk.

A new play by Sutton Vane, whose *Outward Bound* had been so
great a success, was offered on a 'By Arrangement' basis and I was
glad to accept it to occupy the theatre while preparing the next
production. The play was *Overture* and was cast from the rest of
the Everyman company with some additions. It did not have any
of the qualities of *Outward Bound* and was taken off in the second
week, again leaving the theatre empty.

The next new play was *The Swallow* by Viola Tree who proposed, in fact stipulated, that it should be produced by Gerald du
Maurier. Although he lived in Hampstead within a stone throw
of the Everyman, and must have passed it every time he went to
the West End, he had never been in the building nor shown the
remotest interest. I thought the two names would conjure an
audience and add *éclat* to our modest theatre. The first and third
Acts were set in typical stockbroker land. The middle and
romantic act was set in Venice. It soon transpired that du Maurier's
way of working was not our way and the company became
fractious. Tense moments arose, as when Leslie Banks had to
make love to the very beautiful and desirable Hilda Moore. He
did not satisfy du Maurier's idea of expression for it.

du Maurier: "Let's have more passion . . . make me feel you
want her."
Banks (exasperated at the stupidity): "By God, I do."
du Maurier: "Then kiss her, bite her, DO something."
Banks (despairingly): "Sir Gerald, you may bite a woman and
get away with it. I don't . . . and can't." And stalked off the
stage.

Eventually it was arranged that du Maurier would continue to
produce the Stockbroker Acts and I would do the middle romantic act. These conditions produced a sterile result instead of the
life we always tried to give to performances, and the play showed
up as little more than a novel setting to the eternal triangle,
hamstrung by too much talk of golf at Sunningdale and too much
fascism in Venice. It had to be withdrawn in four days.

These three withdrawals entailed too many weeks of closed

Low Tide. 1924
opposite: Illus. 12 Claude Rains and Ivor Barnard
over-page: Illus. 13 Claude Rains and Olive Sloane in the
'knock-out' scene   *Photographs by* 'Sasha'
(See page 65)

theatre and consequently heavy losses by the standing weekly costs such as staff salaries and wages, advertising positions, sundry running costs, not to mention the accumulating rent.

Chesterton's *Magic* had been done by the Summer 'Commonwealth' of the company in 1923: as there had been enquiries for it since it seemed good to repeat it, although it was a play I was never enthusiastic about. Harcourt Williams played the Stranger and produced the play for me. It had a gratifying success. There was even some talk of a transfer to the West End but I could not convince myself to risk that.

Interest in the American dramatist Eugene O'Neill had been growing in London. C. B. Cochran had brought over from New York *Anna Christie* with Pauline Lord. And as Leslie Banks was with the company again and Jean Cadell was available *Diff'rent* was revived; this time with another of the one-act plays from the Volume *Moon of the Carribees* named *The Long Voyage Home*. This made the fourth O'Neill to have its English première at the Everyman.

I had been planning to do *The Wild Duck* which to me is perhaps Ibsen's most interesting play, and I had bespoke Miss Angela Baddeley to play Hedvig. The three misfires in the Spring had disturbed me: I was 'off my stride' and, although I did not know it until later, was heading for a major operation. So when Miss Sybil Arundale made a proposal to take on the theatre for the summer for a season of plays that included Pirandello's *Henry IV*, T. W. Robertson's *Caste* and Goldoni's *Mirandolina*, performed by members of the Everyman company with additions for particular plays, it was easy to come to an arrangement for *The Wild Duck* to be the first presentation. After that I would take a long rest and get myself fit for the Autumn Season. The play opened on the last day of June with a cast exceptionally right in every part, including that most difficult part of Hedvig. Miss Anglea Baddeley gave a performance so simply beautiful and moving that years and years afterwards it is impossible to speak of it without a choke in the voice. The press gave reviews of the play and the performances that were both seriously and warmly written: better could not be asked for.

I went away to my timber hutment in the Chilterns and rested; the kidney pains eased; one of the Doddington sons looked after me. I began to build my dream house in chalk concrete, a simple

The Painted Swan. 1925
back-page: Illus. 14 Acts I & III. *opposite: Illus.* 15 Act II
(See page 71) These sets show the use of the
variable proscenium arch

and cheap method not practised for some hundreds of years. Doddington played house-boy in the mornings and in the afternoons helped to mix concrete with an oldish villager, a good companion and great worker. I read scripts and made selections for the Autumn. It was essential to find an early winner to meet the pressing demands for rent arrears and other accounts. Meantime, Miss Arundale was meeting difficulties and, in spite of the suggestions by critics, not securing a transfer of important plays. She followed my bad example and presented more popular plays which, on the whole, got good notices, largely because of the attractive casts, but countered by summer weather, limited audiences. It is probable that when people made that dreadful lift ascent and surfaced at Hampstead in sunshine they made straight for the Heath and fresh air rather than be broiled in our single-roof battery. Miss Arundale's Season finished rather abruptly at the end of September, and the theatre remained closed until my Autumn opening in mid-October with Ibsen's *Ghosts*.

There had been several requests through the 'Friends' for *Ghosts* to be put on. This is one of three perennially popular plays, the others being *A Doll's House* and *Candida*, that I do not enjoy, but could not reject entirely. I asked Milton Rosmer to produce it for me and he made the best production of the play I have seen. Mrs. Alving was played by Irene Rooke, "superbly throughout", Oswald by Ernest Milton who "has a genius for overdoing things". There was strong audience interest and it played to very good houses for its allotted three weeks.

I was closely involved in arrangements for a play that I hoped would be the essential money-spinner and therefore asked Rosmer also to produce the next play *The Dark Angel* by Guy Bolton, but it involved me in one of my tussles with the Lord Chamberlain. The play was a variation on the war-time theme of soldier on leave and the girl he promises to marry. The curtain rises on a hotel bedroom, a man asleep in it and at the window a girl watching for the dawn to waken him to catch his train back to his Regiment. He is to be killed in the trenches almost as soon as he gets back. This was, in fact, a very sincere and affecting short scene and a common enough story at the time. But—a bed —a girl—and a man all in the same room at the same time? There was a flat refusal for a Licence of any kind. When nearing dress rehearsal stage a message came from St. James's Palace asking me to go and see Lord Cromer. Helpfully but guardedly the difficulty was discussed. He had no other objection to the play, in fact he seemed to like it, and if the bed was moved off-stage into a dressing-room, so that the man could not be seen until he spoke, that would be all right. Eventually I asked "if the bed was not actually in the room but in a sort of alcove" could I have the Licence. To this Lord Cromer agreed with the warning "Mind you, someone will be there on the first night to see". I had an idea for a solution but, wanting a second round of ammunition, I asked that some representative should come with me to see something that was germane. This was granted, and I took an ex-Army Major in a taxi to Shaftesbury Avenue where, outside the Palace Theatre, I showed him a large photograph of a charming young actress in her underwear, lying on a settee, and leaning over her uxoriously, the leading man. "Ah! Yes." said the Army, "but they don't do it in the performance." "Do what?" I asked. Quickly he slid into the taxi and was gone. I returned to Hampstead and instructed the carpenters to form a stage-wide arch and drop it into the set, hiding the head of the bed but not the lower half. Not a move, not a thing, was altered. The bed was technically off-stage and the man was first seen sitting on the edge pulling on his riding-boots.

The Dark Angel was no masterpiece but was a sincere and touching little play on a genuine but unpopular human problem. It was, however, more a West-End play than an Everyman type and not being of particular interest to our audience was taken off after two weeks. This gave a useful freedom for preparing the next production *Sweet Pepper* which I hoped would prove the much-needed transfer to the West End. *Sweet Pepper* was a best-seller romantic novelette set in Budapest. Girl secretary falling for the high-life of British officers, Hungarian aristocrats, Gipsy music and all the excitements that Budapest can indeed give. It had sold untold thousands across America. The middle act was a party set in the apartment of Count Tibor Arkozi and for this scene I had brought over a genuine Gipsy Orchestra of five, including a Zimbalon. The sensuous heart-searching of the old gipsy music by the violins almost saved the play. Music like this had never been heard in London and people were enraptured, applauding excitedly.

The author warned me of the gipsies' drinking habits and to

ensure them being not only present but sufficiently correct when required for performance. Accordingly they were made to report at the theatre at 5.30 each day and were then locked in a room with an appropriate quantity of alcohol until due on stage. Thus they were properly mellowed, neither too sober nor too inebriated to play. A number of engagement for them to play at private 'musical parties' had been fixed for them at fees of £100 a time.

The author had been obdurate about the sanctity of his version but, on the performance and the notices, recognised that drastic adjustments were essential. The theatre was closed for a week to make these but it was now too late and after a further week it was taken off.

Now occurred an opportunity to apply an idea I had long advocated: the interchange of companies with the main repertory companies in the provinces. None of them so far had accepted but now William Armstrong, the very successful Director of the Liverpool Playhouse, who had previously been a member of the Everyman company, proposed a play and a date. *Inheritors* by the American authoress Susan Glaspell (whose one-act *Suppressed Desires* at the Everyman in 1921 had been her introduction to the English stage) was brought, with their own scenery, for two weeks. This was an entirely successful venture and would have been repeated by Armstrong and myself in the following year. Many years after, I noted with interest, that repertory and civic theatres began to realise the value of company interchange.

Now with very mixed feelings I entered on my next, and last, production. At the year end Foster had given me formal notice that unless the total arrears of rent, at the increased rates, were paid up my tenancy would terminate at the end of January. A stage version of G. K. Chesterton's novel *The Man who was Thursday* had been made by Mrs. Cecil Chesterton and Ralph Neale and approved by G.K.C. and it had been sent to me. Some adjustments were discussed and made: scenically it was still very tricky but by adopting some of the newer continental practices and with a trick or two of our own the difficulties were rather 'magically' overcome. Neither critics nor audience understood what the author was getting at but enjoyed the performance none the less. The critics wrote long dissertations on "Chesterton's philosophic symbolism"; the audience just ignored any parable and, led by the "Author's chuckles which shook the theatre like the passing of a Tube Train", delightedly enjoyed its "glorious fun". Even James Agate, whose praise was hard to come by wrote "The piece is extremely well acted by a company whose names it is a pleasure to write down. . . . The impressionist production was as stimulating as anything I have seen in a London theatre. . . . Who would have thought that the feeling of a roysterer's tavern could be so perfectly rendered by three bits of painted cardboard and the device of two sailors sitting motionless nose to nose."

For Everymaniacs there were added amusements. I had already known the pleasure of helping his wife to extricate Chesterton from one of those abominable narrow-doored carriages that used to run on the Beaconsfield Line (she pushed from inside while I pulled at his black "Inverness" from the platform till he came out like a champagne cork). So, when Chesterton came to a rehearsal it was realised that he could not settle his immense quarters into *one* of our stalls. For the first night we took out the adjoining arms between two seats and gave him an ample fauteuil in which he rolled about shouting with delighted laughter thereby adding greatly to the pleasure of the audience.

Finale: 1926

The Man who was Thursday could have had a transfer to the West End but I was in no position to negotiate. Success though it was, it was barred from even the customary three weeks. My notice terminated at the end of January and I had to get out; even the scenery was impounded as part of my assets to meet rent.

It was claimed that around £3,500 was due to Mr. Foster for unpaid balance of rent, and there was about £1,500 of trading liabilities, a normal amount for which we were under no pressure. To protect the trading creditors I went into voluntary bankruptcy, on legal advice but against the advice of my accountants who urged that a meeting of creditors should be called and a scheme for continuance prepared. It was all too late, even for the public appeal for funds for which the *Daily Telegraph* was prepared to open its columns.

On the announcement of the termination of my management the dramatic critics seemed to be genuinely disturbed. "His work at Hampstead entitles him to the admiration of all serious lovers of the theatre and his departure is an occasion for deep regret." "It might seem a matter for despair." "Though a small theatre and salaries running low there has been more good acting at Hampstead in his reign than in any single big London Theatre." "Pioneer of the 'Little Theatre' Movement in London." One columnist summed up the reaction as: "The Critics have, in fact, suddenly become quite sentimental about the matter and many who have been distinctly severe on Mr. MacDermott in the past are now explaining what splendid work he has done for all the world as if they were writing an obituary."

On the Monday morning as I stood under the archway waiting for a taxi to take me, and all the belongings I was allowed in two suitcases, I could hear my successors already at work in the theatre. These new tenants were a group of three, my Business-Manager, my Stage-Manager and Raymond Massey. Without any word to me they had negotiated with Mr. Foster and had been granted a Tenancy at the original rate of £10 a week. They commenced full of promise and convinced that they could make a fortune where I had failed. They dwindled out by the end of the year.

A partnership between Milton Rosmer and Malcolm Morley followed in June, 1927. In spite of Rosmer's great ability as both actor and producer this venture also lasted a short time. I happened to meet Miss Irene Rooke (Mrs. Milton Rosmer) one day in Great Portland Street. She said ". . . but its a drain. Money pours down it." There followed sundry ventures of shrinking repute till the day came for *The Everyman Revue*. I treasure the programme which was sent to me many years later. The Revue included *The Girls, Meeting the Wife, Taking the dog for a walk, Happy to be alive in a Can-Can Dance* and a final *Personally I love you.* The local papers let themselves go on this: "Brows are being worn low this Season. No more Nordic Gloom; Italian Expressionism; nor Spanish Poesy. Instead noisy gaiety; blaring Jazz; and barking dogs."

Milton Rosmer left the partnership in March, 1929, and Malcolm Morley carried on alone. In November, 1929, he organised the Everyman Theatre Guild and during this time was responsible for the first English production of Ostrovsky's *The Storm*, and also for *Ghosts*, in which Sybil Thorndike appeared, among others.

Malcolm Morley left in 1931 and the lease of the theatre was bought from Mr. Foster by Miss Consuelo de Reyes of Citizen House, Bath, where she had a small private theatre and staged short plays of a religious character with amateur actors. Some of these were put on at the Everyman which she used as a vacation School of Drama. Eventually the theatre was acquired by Mr. Fairfax-Jones and converted into a Film Theatre showing continental and other films that were anathema to 'the Trade'. Gradually with skill and perseverance he built up the Everyman into the most interesting of the specialised cinemas in London which has been kept alive and challenging to the present day.

THE EPILOGUES

Setting the Play
Directing the Play
Finance

Setting the Play

The choice of scenic method at the Everyman was enforced by financial stringency, and the fact that we were to present some fifteen different plays in each year. Clearly a strictly practical and economic system had to be worked out and in any case, before this could be adopted, we were faced, in the first three-month experimental season, with the same restrictions on materials that had hampered the building conversion. Scene canvas, for instance, which is of a special quality and width, was unobtainable; even the scenery-contracting firms could get only an occasional bolt. I well remember the triumph of our scene-painter, H. W. Craven, arriving with the end part of a roll that he had persuaded a West-End carpenter to let him have.

We had to devise substitutes, and the army ablutions-shed was recruited into further use. The asbestos sheets were mounted on frames of hangar-timber remaining from the auditorium flooring. In *The Tragedy of Nan* they were used wooden-frame side forward to form a half-timber set; used asbestos-side forward they formed the Spanish house-setting for *The Bonds of Interest*. Their weight made serious difficulties for the men when making any scene-change during the play.

War-disposal balloon-fabric came on the market about this time. The English variety was of a coarse weave and unsuitable, but the French fabric made from a form of silk was admirable and cheap, under ten shillings a yard, and this was used in place of scene-canvas as well as by the wardrobe for the costumes designed by Randolph Schwabe for the Shakespeare plays. There was a wide range of rich and of subtle colours and his costumes, deservedly, caused some stir.

The first and rigid rule of our scene-building system was that every piece must conform to a scale of measurement based on multiples of one foot, so that every piece had a width of one, three or six feet. Thus they were easily interchangeable, and would build into solid patterns of walls, windows, fireplaces, bookcases, doorways. They were, of course, all of a uniform height, but contrary to West-End custom their bottom-rails were all at right-angles to the sides. This was possible because, intentionally, the stage had been built with a level surface and no rake. West-End stages had all been built sloping from back to front, essential if the stalls audience were to see artistes full-length to their feet. The Everyman reversed this by its sharply raked auditorium floor, an innovation to London. The basic scene-pieces could therefore be placed anywhere on stage; on either side, up or down, angled across, to any pattern noted on an author's or a producer's design. This inter-changeability was invaluable. The basic pieces were a set of round-headed arches each with a pilaster on one side. When these were assembled on stage the space of the arch could be left as an opening or window or could be filled-in by wall-pieces or door-pieces, or the like. The result can be seen in *Romeo and Juliet* contrasted with *Arms and the Man* and *The Man of Destiny*. The pilasters masked any joins of the pieces. The pieces filling-in were all to the standard measurements and were held in position by large turn-buttons. To change one scene to another was simple and quick by unbuttoning one set of filling pieces and replacing with others stacked ready. The filling pieces were plain for wall-surfaces, or might incorporate door-frames or windows, bookcases and so on; all had true-mouldings round them which again masked the joins with the door or window sash. The result gave a solidity seldom achieved by the customary method.

Later a set of arch-pieces was added, with level tops to the openings and fluted, instead of plain, pilasters. These were used in *The Mask and the Face* and in *Home Affairs*. The same over-door pediment was used in a street set in white in *The Lost Silk Hat* and in mahogany in a palladian interior in *The Painted Swan*. Such a piece of a fireplace or a doorway might be in use in one set on Saturday night at the end of a run and with a coat of another colour be on stage in a different setting on Sunday for dress-rehearsal of another play. Change of colour, position, angle and lighting would make it unrecognisable.

Meantime there had been also an important addition to stock. This was a set of black velvet curtains filling the whole stage. They were bought second-hand after use in one of William Poel's mediaeval curtain-settings. At the end of the war the German theatre had little money at current values to spend on new settings and there was much experiment with grey and black velvet hung stages. Some magnificent effects were obtained, and this was another economic method I was anxious to adopt. If a stage is hung completely with black velvet curtains and something light-coloured, such as a costume, a chair, placed before them, and only that object is lit, the audience will see only the object. This made possible very rapid scene-changes and numerous sets in one play. In *Low Tide*, for instance, the dock-side warehouse yard was set near back stage and the black curtains run across in front of it. On front-stage was placed the mean attic room formed from folding screens. When lit nothing was to be seen but the room. At the knock-out punch of Olive Sloane by Claude Rains, all light was blacked-out; the screens were folded off and the table removed; the black curtains were drawn off, and the blue sky lighting swelled-up. The change took seconds only and the fore-curtain was not even closed. The same use was made in *The Man who was Thursday*. Another useful innovation was the variable proscenium which could be reduced in width or in height merely by pulling on marked sets of ropes off-stage. When the feel of a small room or place was required it was most valuable.

The screens used for the attic room were the famous white folding screens of Gordon Craig for *Hamlet* which we were fortunately able to buy cheap. They were each 2 ft. wide and 22 ft. high, in folds of four. They were very heavy and clumsy to handle. We cut them in half, making sets of 2 ft. wide by 11 ft. high and used them frequently for small and intimate rooms. In *Low Tide* they were covered with a cheap attic wallpaper and for *The Painted Swan* second setting they were given a wash of light grey-green.

Two round free-standing columns were built, covered in battleship-linoleum: these were used on the forestage at the sides of the proscenium for *Twelfth Night* and also appeared in the palladian first-act of *The Painted Swan*. With these, a set of four collapsible rostrums, a pair of long steps that went the full width of the stage and other steps, all to the standard widths, the scene stock was complete. The rostrums gave varying levels of stage that were of great value in groupings and entrances. With this complete stock of pieces, ready by the end of the second year, we were able to produce a wide variety of settings at the average cost of about £30 per play. The pieces had an undercoat of light grey over which would be put a wash of white or white tinted with "dutch-pink" (which isn't pink but yellow), or shades of grey. This ground colour was 'painted' with light, which might be changed with the mood of a scene, and gave an infinitely greater subtlety than could be got by any paint or distemper.

Lighting was to be one of our chief innovations. There were no footlights at the Everyman. This is commonplace to-day but in the 1920's was revolutionary. Normally a stage was flooded with a blaze of white light and artistes had to put on heavy make-up to counteract the lack of natural shadow, under the eyebrow for instance, that resulted from the upward glare from the footlights, which also had the effect of throwing their shadows on the upper part of walls, or of skies and buildings in open-air scenes. For face-lighting, instead of footlights, the Everyman had initially two banks of large flood-lamps, one on each side of the auditorium a third-way back from the stage and three more hung from the roof in a central position. This was effective but unsightly. Later, with a four-figure gift from a most loyal supporter, I went to Germany and bought a complete set of the Phoebus system of modern lighting including a lever control bank with dimmers that were a miracle of smoothness, and caused envious comment from even highly technical electrical engineers who came to see them. The installation included one outsize lamp which was christened 'Big Bertha' after the famous German gun of the war period. Its interior was lined with reflecting mirrors and, with its condensers and lenses, its total output full-up was 26,000 candle-power. It was in fact a modified searchlight, and was hung on the wall right at the back of the auditorium. It was the remarkable gradation control by its dimmer that so much impressed the engineers. All other lamps were removed from the auditorium and the light from 'Big Bertha' was precisely trimmed to fall on stage within the proscenium frame. The source of light was not now noticeable to the audience, and the angle of fall threw the artistes' shadows below knee-height and thus among furniture, furnishings and carpet where they were never noticed. Even with a wide night sky of deep blue no shadow was to be seen.

One important innovation was the 'Sky'. I wanted to avoid the clothy dullness of the usual painted canvas in standard use. The gable wall that formed the back of the stage was first wired in three circuits of fifty or more torchlamps for stars controlled by three switches on the electrical control-board. Then it was rendered all over with a half-inch coat of cement. When nearly dry, but not 'set', three men rapidly punched it all over with road-sweepers' coarse brooms leaving a myriad of tiny holes. Left to harden, it was sprayed overall with a thin coat of white; then, with the spray directed upward, with a light green; finally, with the spray directed downward, a coat of light blue. By this method the thousands of minute holes formed by the broom were given mottled coats on their 'roofs' of pale green over white and their depths and 'floors' of blue over white. It was lit from above by a bank of special lamps with fronts of frosted heat-resisting glass of different blues and some greens. Right across stage, two feet from the bottom of the sky, a sunken trough was formed and in it were set a dozen to fifteen flood-lamps throwing upwards deep blue at left and right followed by pink, then ambers, with a few plain white frosted glass in the centre. The sky holes responded to the colour thrown at them and the greatest subtlety of gradation could be obtained from light blue summer sky, through a pink-amber-red sunset to deep night blue sky with stars showing, by moving appropriate dimmers in counterpoint. These changes could be made in minutes or spread over the full length of an act. This latter effect was used in *The Man who was Thursday*, when another sunset trick faded out a row of poplars that stood out black against the day-sky.

One other advantage of 'Big Bertha' should be recorded. By using a selection of small flood-lamps, baby-spots, etc. for general lighting, one part of a room or position such as a chair or the model's rostrum in Dubedat's studio could be given added significance for some important passage or action without inter-fering with the face lighting. A story about 'Big Bertha' may not be amiss here. With its light carefully graded, artistes needed less and less make-up. The natural shadows and lines of the face made for greater subtlety of expression. They could only arrive at correct make-up under direction because they could not see themselves under its light. When it was first put into use there were complaints from them that they were being under-lit. After a few performances the stage-manager brought me a message from one difficult member, who was shortly to leave the company, that he would not go on for his scene in the last act unless there was full light. On the principle of you can lead me but you can't push me, I picked up my inter-com and called the switchboard. For the last act, I said, you will bring 'Big Bertha' up to full capacity and you will not reduce it except on a direct instruction from me. Then I went down to the stage. At the act end the company came off with their eyes streaming and unable to orientate themselves. I told them of the threat conveyed to me and the instruction I had given to the electrician . . . and had no more trouble about lighting. But the actor in question had a rough time from the company.

Before leaving the subject of scenery, I must pay tribute to the stage-crew who were with me from before the opening until my last day, except the carpenters, who changed with notable regularity, and the first electrician, Veness, who transferred to Basil Dean and was set-up later as a subsidiary of Reandean to supply stage equipment. Of the invaluable Martin I have already written. Even when he became chief electrician he continued to be boiler-man, caretaker, and the man one turned to in any emergency. He had an attractive little daughter, who developed a mastoid that was never completely cured: this reduced him to a state of extreme worry and depression but he never allowed it to interfere with his job. I like to believe that the satisfaction he found in the Everyman was some compensation to him for other unhappiness in his life.

Craven was also a man of many parts. He was a son of the great Hawes Craven, the scene-painter. Craven also had been to sea and had lost an eye which was replaced by an old-fashioned glass eye. He was property-maker and master, but early in the story also took over the scene painting. He went to endless trouble to mix paints to satisfy my severe demands of colour and tone. His painting was mostly done during the nights at change-over weekends. At three or four o'clock in the morning his glass eye and the dust would have irritated the surrounding skin and tears would be flowing down one side of his face as he brought me still another colour-sample. I, at my most insistent, would reject it. Still, with a smile, Craven would say "Excuse a moment, Sir" and walk up into a dark corner of the stage where with a forefinger he dug out the glass eye and returned saying "Alright now till morning, Sir" and go off with his bucket to the workshop to produce still another sample. A worthy fellow to Martin.

Finch, our regular Commissionaire, whose tact and efficiency in handling cars and late-comers, enraged because they were too late to be allowed into the auditorium, was unfailing and won us many friends. Hawkswell, slow, lumbering, unfailingly willing; and Mrs. Doddington whose husband had been killed in a war-time explosion leaving her to bring up a brood of sons each of whom as they came of working age was joined to the Everyman staff in one capacity or another. They lived in the tenement buildings and Mrs. D. brooded over all of us; made tea and her own-baked scones; cooked meals for me or for Miss Kent when we worked overnight; did washing or sewing for any or all Everymaniacs. I hope she got as much satisfaction from mothering us as we had comfort from her ministrations.

Directing the Play

At the turn of this century the English theatre was dominated by the actor-manager under whom no independent producer's function was recognised. The chief aim of any presentation was the enhancement of one individual actor and occasionally his wife: all other characters in a play served only as foils. To this end masterpieces of the English drama were re-shaped and re-written; speeches and telling lines were transferred from other characters and even from other plays; matter was written-in; in pursuit of personal aggrandisement performances were buried under magnificence of costume and the stage was overloaded with vulgar extravagance of painted scenery. Artists were commissioned because they were fashionable painters.

But the end of the actor-manager system was already in sight, hastened by Bernard Shaw's devastating criticisms in the *Westminster Gazette* before the outbreak of the Great War. Rumours had been reaching discriminating playgoers of the revolution that had taken place in the continental theatre. Plays of the Scandinavian authors began to be published in translations; then the Germans from Hebbel to Hauptmann; the Belgian Maeterlinck; some Russians, but not yet Chekhov, nor the French writers for the theatres of Antoine, Gémier and Copeau. There was renewed interest in our own Jacobean playwrights and in the ancient Greek dramatists. A trickle of news followed about the totally different organisation of the continental playhouses, particularly of the Germans. First of the 'neue Shakespeare Buhne' simplified manner of presenting the plays; then of the new bowl-shaped steeply-raked auditoriums with no galleries, devised by the architect Littman; of the new methods of lighting by the Italian–Swiss Adolph Appia; followed by the simplified beauty and dignity of the scenic settings, partly influenced by Gordon Craig, and the ease of scene-changing brought into practice by the mechanising and pre-setting of platform stages with off-stage 'docks'. Finally came information about heavy endowment by States, Municipalities and Workers Unions that enabled these theatres to maintain permanent companies of actors and to appoint directors to maintain the highest standards in the choice of plays; select the actors to perform them; and to develop imagination in their presentation.

The only approximation to these ideals the London public had seen were the brief Vedrenne–Barker Seasons and the occasional appearances of the Dublin Abbey Theatre Company. This blossoming of the Irish literary renaissance in the poetic plays of Synge, of Yeats, and of the peasant plays and dialect comedies of Lady Gregory and others, was the more impressive because the players started as a group of part-time actors who, by day, earned their keep in dull occupations but, by their passionate integrity and the sensitivity of their playing together, won world-fame for their performances.

Names of the new masters of Direction became known— Stanislavsky, Meyerhold, Reinhardt, Gémier, Copeau and some of the Americans working in their Universities' 'Greek-style' theatres that developed into the American 'Little Theatre Movement'.

From all this, at the end of the war, the new concept of the producer-in-charge became acceptable in London and playgoers looked to him to bring to them a simple, dignified presentation of plays that would promote the interchange between audience and stage that is the ultimate satisfaction of theatre. But there was still no committed theatre available and the audience for such plays was hardly satisfied by the single membership performances on Sundays of the Stage Society, the Pioneer Players and the like. Performances for the general public on Sundays were totally banned by the Lord Chamberlain's and the London County Council's Licence. With all theatres standing empty it was possible to borrow one for a nominal fee or for 'costs entailed' for staff, light and heat. Occasionally a Monday matinée might be added.

More important for the future of drama were the so-called Repertory Theatres established in a few of the larger provincial cities, Birmingham, Manchester, Liverpool, Glasgow. Misuse of the word repertory, however, masked a number of the short-comings of these ventures. It gave the impression that, as on the continent, such theatres held a stock of productions that could be brought out of store in sequence to satisfy varying audience demands; that the playing company would be permanent and of all-round excellence; and that working together over a period they would study the plays in depth between rehearsal, and thus naturally give subtle and finished performances. The Dublin Abbey Theatre working in exactly this manner seemed to provide evidence. But the majority of the English so-called Repertory Theatres did not work in this way. Faced with the limited number of serious playgoers in each town they became, in fact, little more than one-week short-run 'stock' companies which, presenting a different play each week, could not possibly give studied interpretations. The mere learning of each week's cargo of speaking lines was an accomplishment, but depth was impossible. It is greatly to their credit that with less than a full week to prepare the new, while performing the old for six nights and a matinée, they put on such performances as they did.

In the years following the end of the first world war a new type of management had developed in the London theatre. Many buildings had fallen into the hands of a limited number of brick-and-mortar owners who did not themselves present plays but leased their theatres to play-presenting hit-and-miss managements. This had one advantage: the business man, not being an artist himself, had to interpose someone between himself and the artistes of the performing company and so opened the way for emergence of the producer-function. Nothing merely 'happens' on a stage: from the selfishness of the actor-manager to the inspired lunacies of the Crazy Gang, somebody at sometime has to 'arrange' the traffic of the stage and it was eventually recognised that something more than stage-management was essential.

It was at this stage and in this environment that the project of the Everyman Theatre was launched. It was intended to adopt as much of the continental system as was practicable on the restricted funds and the materials then available; and a number of distinctive features that directly affect producing were incorporated. Its steeply-raked auditorium floor gave a clear view of the stage from every seat; the stage was level and not raked as customary in England; it had a variable proscenium-opening and a shallow projecting fore-stage; lastly it had an imported German lighting installation with separate dimmers for every circuit and no foot-lights. It had a permanent company of artistes and of staff; it had

91

its own workshops for scene-making adjacent to the stage, and it had provision for property-making and for wardrobe. It was the first London theatre open to the general public where a director-producer was in overall control of policy and production. The acting company was built up with artistes in full accord with all aspects of its policy who were prepared, indeed anxious, to contribute towards the new venture by committing themselves to work solely for it and at the very modest salaries it could offer in contrast to their usual West-End earnings. Ideally a producer should be installed in his own theatre and I was indeed fortunate to find myself so placed in effect, even though some of the provisions were extremely modest. I was to be assisted in overcoming the slovenliness of speech, only too prevalent on the London stage at that time, by an expert in voice production. And to bring artistes' individual movement to the equivalent beauty of, for instance, Copeau's company, one of the leading Dalcroze* teachers was engaged. Unfortunately one or two of the older, more experienced artistes showed resentment at being 'sent back to school' and made it difficult for other members to give time to the sessions. Moreover the experts were not always tactful in dealing with the refractory. Money for these supplemental assistants became hard to find and, eventually, with the engagement of Miss Edith Craig with her all-round talent, these appointments were allowed to lapse.

During the time of conversion of the Drill Hall the first four of the selected plays were studied and scripts prepared; the main parts of the company were gathered and told the parts they would be asked to play; the scenery was designed and put under construction in the workshops. When the theatre was ready to open three of these plays planned to be in repertory for the first three months experimental season were in varying stages of rehearsal and scenery, costumes, etc. were ready. The fourth was on the stocks.

Of these plays three had been previously produced in London or in repertory theatres and most members of the company had played in them. With the workshops immediately adjacent, the producer or stage-manager could frequently inspect and confer

* Dalcroze Eurythmic method of music exposition was then in highest repute and in the theatre its disciplines could be invaluable, especially for concerted movement.

with the working staff to settle the many queries that arose during construction. Scene-detail, paint-colour, costume-material were under continuous supervision and collaboration. The time-saving was incalculable, and rehearsals progressed with reasonable smoothness.

It was not long, however, before I realised a serious short-coming in myself; that, simply stated, I did not have the practical working experience necessary for handling rehearsals of a play. I was diffident, hesitant and cripplingly shy. Facing a group of people highly skilled in the practice of the stage I found it impossible to stop them and jump onto the stage with "No . . . No . . . take it this way".

In theory I knew all that could be known about interpretation, performance, method. I had read everything available in English on the subject, ancient and modern. On my shelves stood Goethe and Schlegel and Brandt; Gordon Craig in bulk; Stanislavsky and Meyerhold; articles by the score about Gémier and Copeau; about the American Little Theatre Movement and its designers and producers, including the Provincetown theatre where later Eugene O'Neill came to life. But to translate all this into the daily traffic of rehearsal was a very different proposition. Moreover I had not then acquired that faculty of command, the air of authority that is learned only by its practice. Furthermore I was of a new school that believed a performance must not be imposed on an artiste but must grow out of his understanding and acceptance of whatever character he is to portray. I believed, and still believe, that when a play is cast the production is half-made and it is for the artiste to develop the detail of his performance from his study and comprehension of the character. The producer's part is to explain, elucidate, encourage; but not to perform every part, give every inflection, demonstrate every move and turn. To do so results in cardboard figures where the portrayal is at variance with the player's own *persona*.

Of my flair for casting I have never had doubt. I remained convinced that I had something of significance to contribute; but I still required to devise the method and practice, the compromise necessary between my theories and my shyness and inexperience.

From most of the company there continued unbroken loyalty to the Everyman venture and also to myself as its instigator. But one or two of the older and more set of the artistes, realising my inexperience and still tending to jockey for their own status and place in the company, began to test both my methods and my authority. I noticed them muttering in corners and at rehearsals, exchanging despairing looks at my mistakes, which only made me flounder the more. I sensed incipient revolt and was appraised of a developing intrigue. Obviously I was faced with the need to make a major personal decision. For the ultimate success of the venture ought I to withdraw entirely and hand over to one or other of the experienced members of the company? Or ought I to consider my contribution of prime importance and remain in control?

Looking critically at the malcontents I could not believe that any of them had it in them to carry both sides of the venture through a period of stress to eventual success. On the other hand, in spite of my limitations, there to be seen was a fully functioning theatre that I had brought into existence, something London had never had before, with enthusiastic audiences, particularly of the younger theatregoers, and rapidly winning recognition and praise from the critics and the press. Eventually I decided on a compromise—*reculer pour mieux sauter*! I would give up producing; learn my job; and fight to overcome the limitations of my shyness, while retaining effective final control.

I was extremely fortunate that at this juncture a practical solution was ready to hand and I was able to engage Edith Craig to produce the first Season of Shaw plays in 1921. Relieved of the daily rehearsal hours, I was able to give closer attention to the general running of the theatre, its workshops, the box office, programmes and cleaning; advertising, printing, publicity; not least to the continuous need for money-raising and devising economies. In the farthest back corner of the auditorium was a single seat, never sold, marked on the box office plan 'D.D.' and known by everyone as the "Dear Director's" or "Damned Driver's" as might be the feeling at the moment. It was here that I spent part of each day, silently in the darkened auditorium, watching Miss Craig at work with the company and, both now and later, other producers I engaged when a fee was available. They included Milton Rosmer, Nicholas Hannen, Komisarjevsky, and still others when the theatre was let briefly for 'try-outs' by other managements.

I observed how these producers differed in their methods; that one came to rehearsal with positions, movements and business plotted in meticulous detail; but that another would have planned only a rough shape and would depend on his inspiration-of-the-moment to fill in the detail. That one would drive the company again and again over some part of a scene, tending to exhaust them by over-long sessions; while another, finding some passage did not 'move' would skip past it, returning later in the hope that the difficulty had run away.

I noted also the quiddities of the artistes. How one would be word-perfect at the third or fourth rehearsal while another would be still clutching the typed-part in his hands at the end of the second week causing despair in those who had to play scenes with him. How one would resist a correction but a second would accept and start straightaway to develop it. How a third, though having no immediate lines in a scene, would contribute to its life by following the dialogue while another would become merely a hole in the picture. I noted too how some still tended to play for their own part instead of to the play as a whole, sidling to centre-stage although their part in a scene might be subsidiary. These, and a score of other 'tricks of the trade', I noted should be checked at once firmly and not hesitantly nor diffidently.

Then I began to think that, whether by some lack in producer or artiste, perhaps merely exasperation or tiredness, some significant or subtle stroke of the author was not given full value, that emotional impact was missed. I began to feel that, excellent as was the work of these producers, the end result when the curtain rose could fall short of the standards the Everyman was intended to secure. Gradually in the ensuing months a set of working principles took shape in my mind and I was comforted to note that none were contrary to the theories I had absorbed from my years of study.

A play is not merely a vehicle for acting and its successful presentation calls for the most intense effort of interpretative insight on the part of a producer. Not only should he feel a lively sympathy with an author's attitude to the subject of his play and to its theme but he must have an instinct alert to subtleties of the author's thought, and of his characters and their interaction. The transposition of an author's work from the printed page to the stage performance calls for exercise of that instinct more alert in some minds than others, and a producer must cultivate it.

Instinct is not enough, however, without technical experience. To feel that a line or a speech must be spoken in a particular way the producer must know why the character's thought or feeling comes forth in precisely that line and must be able to explain to an artiste the approach to it. If the author is alive, and available, there can be fruitful collaboration between him and the producer. Authors have stimulating ideas and, eager to commit them to dialogue, will ignore the simplest of mechanics, of how an actor necessarily at one side of the stage is to get himself to an equally necessary position at the opposite side and what the rest of the characters are to do while he is doing it. If budding playwrights would study the mechanics before writing, much time would be saved.

I warmly commend the example of John van Druten. One evening at the Everyman a young member of our audiences approached me and asked me to let him attend rehearsals. It is well known that producers, artistes, and stage managers intensely dislike admission of outsiders in this way and my first impulse was to refuse the request. But he was persuasive, saying that he meant to write a play and was anxious to learn how actors reacted to the producer and to each other when actually working together. He was convincingly earnest. This made me like him and I agreed, stipulating that he must sit right back in the auditorium and be totally dumb! After some weeks he came to me again asking if he might talk to members of the company to discuss the why and wherefores of exchanges during rehearsal between producer and an artiste or between two artistes working on a scene. Again I agreed. Thereafter he went away and wrote his excellent and very successful first play *Young Woodley*.

The author writes "Pause" and so poses a challenge. The actor will stop speaking. But to achieve the pause, so often mishandled, there must be the preparation for the pause; the speaking-pace before it; the decision how long to hold it; the exact way to break it, whether by change of tone, or by some movement, whether by another character or the first speaker; the speaking-pace and the manner after it.

Or the author writes "Enter" and a character steps into view knowing the bare words to speak but not having studied the 'why' and the 'wherefore' and therefore not the 'how'. Sometimes I would say "Yes . . . but what were you doing five minutes ago before you opened that door . . . because that also is part of your character."

To-day any producer worth his salt knows and practises all this, but in the 1920's it was considered eccentric. One instance of this preparation for entrance will serve also as a tribute to a great actor who first made fame at the Everyman. Watching Claude Rains before he made entry on a scene, he would come on-stage a few minutes before due, in the costume of Napoleon or Dubedat; give a smile of greeting; exchange some whispered joke or by-play with the Stage-Manager. Then the smile would fade; his eyes seem to withdraw inwards; his stance would change; his 'build' would seem to spread into the costume; his face lines would alter and out of his inner comprehension he would draw another mind. Expression new-set he would turn and face the door. Ready. Not Rains: but Napoleon or Dubedat.

Producers vary widely in their methods. Some look on the company as the awkward squad of recruits and impose strict discipline. At the opposite extreme the attitude of others is "whatever you feel, old boy". The good producer lies somewhere between. I do not believe in the strict discipline code as a method in any art. Like service discipline it produces slick efficiency; from curtain rise to curtain fall everything may go without a hitch, but the result is often like tinned-fruit as compared to fresh-grown: the savour has been lost in the processing.

After a year of this apprenticeship, it seemed essential that I should resume the whole job of production. I had to face it: I must overcome my diffidence and put myself again to the test. Marrying theory to observed practice I now set a working basis for myself.

First the play must be read and re-read and again re-read. Then it should be put aside for a time while it works, like a yeast in the mind, until every meaning and implication of the dialogue is understood; and the motive and background of each character analysed. If the author is alive he should be conferred with at this point for elucidation and for any adjustments to be agreed. Next the production-script must be prepared by working through the play scene-by-scene, page-by-page, line-by-line, marking in one margin notes of interpretation, inflection, pace; and in the other all positions, movements, groupings, properties required together with lighting notes and a thousand and one such details.

For this a scale plan of the stage is required and the scene, as visualised in the imagination, marked on it, showing also levels, steps, openings such as doors etc., and any pieces of fixed furniture or special properties. Chess-pawns or dice or round ivory games-counters are required, each marked with the name of a character. Next a bunch of coloured pencils to use different colours for lighting, 'warnings', 'effects', etc. Finally, page-by-page through each scene, moving the character-pieces on and off and about the board as required, and noting each change in a margin, with diagrams of the movements avoiding 'masking' or collisions and having each character in appropriate position at important points in the dialogue. All this in precise detail, prepared to go to first rehearsal with everything 'plotted' subject only to minor adjustments that might seem improvements.

This preparation of a producer's 'Book' is essential: first to enable the producer to keep within his overall picture; next to save valuable time in rehearsals, often wasted by fruitless discussions of seeming snags; lastly, because it is a courtesy to the cast to enable them to rely from the commencement on main movement and grouping, so freeing them to walk their parts as they learn their lines. It also helps to prevent that worst of theatrical tags: "It'll be all right on the night". *It*, whatever *It* is, must be *right* at the earliest moment and firmly set long before final rehearsals.

The artistes at the Everyman were always given a full script of the play not, as then customary, only a typed part with cues. Then came a first-reading, with the complete cast present and the stage-management. This might well take two or more days for giving a general exposition of the style and mood the production was intended to take.

First Rehearsal was again a slow proceeding. With the stage marked out and substitute furniture positioned, the artistes read their lines, took the moves given, and marked their script. After this stringing-the-skeleton artistes or stage-manager might question, or make suggestions, sometimes accepted, usually not. Lastly, I knew I must have patience, and patience, and always patience, together with a determination to have my own way right through to dress-rehearsal, without deflection from my own vision of the play and the feeling it had roused in the first reading.

Finance

There has been so much misconception about the finance of the Everyman and so many statements have been circulated by people, who had some fleeting connection with it but knew nothing of its actual working, that a statement of figures may well cause some critics to reverse their opinions and others to regret hasty judgments.

A few years before the 1914–18 war a small number of repertory theatres had come into existence in provincial cities supported by private money, but in London the one theatre to receive financial endowment was Miss Lilian Baylis's Old Vic which had a small grant from the Education Office in respect of Shakespeare performances to school children at reduced rates of admission.

From the very inception of the Everyman scheme it was contemplated that some form of endowment must be provided and this was planned for in a variety of ways. In the first place, a non-profit-making Limited Liability Company was registered to ensure correct handling of moneys. It was provided that no dividends would be paid on money subscribed and any surplus funds that might accrue from its operations would be used to improve and extend the work. This was stated in a preliminary prospectus, and incorporated in the Articles of Association and the formal prospectus of the Company. Next it was anticipated that the theatre building would be paid for, fully equipped, out of a building fund to be raised. The premises would therefore be rent free. Further it was expected that, on the continental example, rates etc. on the building would be remitted. Finally, it was hoped that supporters would make annual subscriptions to a working fund. It was believed that, in one way and another, an annual endowment rising to around £5,000 could be provided. This, rising eventually to around £7,500, did occur, although not quite in the way anticipated.

Certain of these anticipations were not to be realised. The

strict limitations imposed following the war on the erection of
new buildings, and the similar regulation of permits for building
materials, caused postponement of the plans to build an entirely
new theatre on continental lines. The working capital, gifted or
subscribed for shares in the Company, was sufficient to pay for
the conversion of the bare and dull Drill Hall into an attractive
small theatre fully equipped, but with space only for 300 seats
against the planning in the original model theatre for 600 seats.
The Hampstead Borough Council not only declined to support
the venture but also refused, against expectation, a remission of
rates. Although the end years of the lease of the Hall were
secured for a moderate payment, this entailed a liability for rent
which proved to be the ultimate burden that terminated the
venture.

The supporters responded handsomely in the early years. Sums
varying from £1 to £500 came steadily from this source and when
the newspapers made known the danger of the theatre closing in
the early days, two or three patrons donated sums in four figures.
Most of these supporters, however, came to the theatre on the
first or second nights of new productions and, seeing the seats full
with no empty places, naturally assumed it could pay its way and
eventually endowment in this form dried up. Fortunately, after the
International Season, when I found myself solely responsible, a
new and unexpected factor brought even larger endowment. This
factor was the successful transfer of some plays to the West End
for long runs and substantial profits which were all furrowed, if
I may keep to the metaphor, back into the Everyman account.
None-the-less, a rigid economy had to be practised and this,
together with the artistes' contribution by their acceptance of
moderate salaries, enabled the theatre to be carried on for its
five-and-a-half year's life.

Another adverse factor that the Everyman had to face was that
the London County Council, when eventually agreeing to license
the building for public performances, made a condition that a
Bar Licence for alcoholic drink would not be applied for.
Although I was, at that time, personally teetotal, I was unable to
understand why it was assumed that the audience at a theatre with
a serious policy was more likely to get troublesome than one at a
leg-show or a bedroom farce. We tried to make up for this lack
by serving what became known to critics and public as the best

coffee in London, but it was doubly hard on the critics who had to make their way out into the cold, the rain or snow, to a public-house some two hundred yards away to get their normal sustenance and it says much for their integrity that their judgments remained unaffected and generous.

Experience at the Everyman amply proved the one major financial requirement that an independent experimental theatre must have funds, other than the receipts from sale of seats, in order to finance its own transfers to long-run theatres, thus gaining the whole profit, and not merely a share of the profits, after the resident management has amply covered all its outgoings.

To turn to weekly working figures in some detail. It was an important principle in the scheme that pricing of seats should be kept as low as practicable, and particularly that provision should be made for the admission of students, fellow-artists, and other young people at a price that they could manage regularly. Admission in West-End theatres at that time ranged from Stalls at 10s. 6d. or 12s. 6d. down to so-called Pit Stalls at 2s. 6d. In some theatres there were Galleries at 1s. 6d. Only Stalls or Dress-Circle were bookable in advance, and standing in queues in cold, rain or snow for some hours before even getting into the building abated much of the pleasure, while the uncertainty whether one would get in at all produced nervous tension and, for the unsuccessful, angry frustration. The successful were faced with a laborious climb up innumerable flights of stone stairs to be packed tightly on hard wooden benches with only part of the stage in view. Having suffered these miseries so often myself I was determined the Everyman should not inflict them. In making the conversion of the Drill Hall it was arranged that from every seat there should be a clear view of the stage and it was decided that all seats would be comfortable and be bookable in advance, including those at the lowest price. The charges fixed at opening were:

		£	s.	d.
100 @ 2s. 6d.	(Side Chairs & Back Row Centre)	12	10	0
126 @ 5s. 0d.	(Centre Block)	31	10	0
70 @ 7s. 6d.	(Front Rows)	26	5	0
		£70	5	0

This gave, on paper, a total weekly capacity of £491 15s. od., but that figure could not ever be reached. 'Complimentaries' were very sparsely given but press seats on first-nights, author's seats, a few V.I.P's, accounted for up to 75 not sold. At the end of the first experimental Season of three months in 1920 the allocation of seats for each price was modified to produce a slight increase in the weekly total to £525.

The critics were very considerate about seat allotment. It was then the London custom to send a pair of tickets to, at least, the national daily papers and to the more important provincial papers with offices in London and also to the weekly journals. Additional tickets might be expected for fashion reporters, art magazines, 'glossies' and their cartoonists. After explanation about our limited capacity, most editors and critics accepted a single seat for the first night or alternately two for the second. This was doubly important in that it helped to keep a reasonable balance between playgoers and critics in the house at one time. Members of the 'Friends of the Everyman' were conceded the right to book for new productions a week in advance of the general booking but no price concession was given except to groups of students and associated socièties who could book blocks of seats at a small reduction.

No further change in prices was made until the opening of the International Season. By that time the repute of the theatre for the high standard of its productions was well established. Under pressure of finance, to try to reduce the gap between income and running costs, a new range of charges was announced. The front five rows of stall were increased to 9s. and the side-chairs, reluctantly, to 3s., giving a paper total for seven performances of £568. This had an unexpected result, for while it made a substantial difference in the case of a very popular success playing to capacity audiences, it actually reduced the returns from any play three-quarters full because by this time our regulars had decided, quite rightly, that the middle rows were the best viewing position, being neither too near the stage nor far enough away to affect the intimacy that was a feature of the theatre. The front stalls were therefore never fully booked until the middle had been sold out. One or two gossip-paragraphists printed objections to the new pricing. One seemed to believe that anything a mile or so from Piccadilly Circus must be correspondingly less good and should therefore be cheaper, even though at that time our highest price was still more than 25 per cent less than in any West End theatre. Another critic, quite hysterically, alleged 'profiteering' and demanded seats at 1s. "as in certain first class West-End theatres", contending that the humbler and often more intelligent playgoer was not sufficiently catered for at the Everyman, but failing to remind his readers of the contrast between queuing, climbing heavenwards, and packing on plain hard benches in those theatres, with the comfortable separate chairs, perfect view of the stage, carpeted floor and, above all, the advance booking, available at the Everyman.

The number of seats available for sale was also reduced when the forestage was used, as for the Shakespeare plays, and when space for an orchestra was required in productions such as *Prunella*, and *The Pedlar's Basket*. At matinées the attendance was poor even during popular seasons like the Shaw. Thus the maximum total could never be reached. Even with the smash hits waiting transfer to the West End such as *At Mrs. Beam's*, *The Mask and the Face*, *Outward Bound*, *Home Affairs*, *The Vortex*, the highest-ever figure for a week was £528, in spite of telephone clamour and optimistic groups in the foyer hoping for returned tickets. The highly popular Shaw Seasons gave very satisfactory averages over their three-monthly periods but the poor matinées limited the weekly totals. As the more expensive seats were the last to be sold, an audience of 75 per cent capacity would show a marked reduction on the total money taken.

The transfers to the West End became the financial lifeline, although the share of profit from them never equalled the inspired guesses of paragraphists and the many rumours of the fortune I was said to be making. Those transfers had to be made by arrangement with a resident management in one or other West-End theatre and not unnaturally they made sure that they collected the lion's share of the receipts. After deduction of their standing costs, there would be a division of the 'Nett' on a roughly fifty-fifty basis. Out of my portion I had to meet author's royalties; company salaries (at West-End rates), etc. All circumstances considered, I found the managements I dealt with scrupulously fair but the nett profit to me was at most only two-thirds of what it could have been if direct transfer on a rental basis could have been obtained. The weekly cheques for my share from such transfers were paid direct into the Everyman account and thus, with other supplementary income in the second part of its life, the Everyman had an endowment varying from about £4,000 to £7,000 each year.

But what happened at the Everyman when the play was not received enthusiastically by the critics? Disaster. And even when critics gave excellent notices to a play, if its subject were of low life, or a problem truthfully and earnestly treated, audiences simply vanished. A first-week might take only around £100, and the second week drop to £15, £8, and on one outstanding occasion to £4 10s.

The drastic drop of receipts was not accompanied by any corresponding drop in costs which varied slightly with the number in the cast, the number of scenes, and minor costs: the average was about £400 per week, with a possible £500, but never less than £325. This is shown by the following typical weekly figures averaged over a number of weeks at the different periods:

(A) Opening Season

(B) Middle Period

(C) Final Year

Items	(A) £	(B) £	(C) £
RENT	10	20	30 plus %
Insurances etc.	2	2	2
PUBLICITY	65	65	65
Advertising, Newspapers, Tubes & Buses, Posters etc., Circulars & Postages			
AUTHORS' ROYALTIES *ca.*	20	25	25
ARTISTES' SALARIES *ca.*	110	180	220
STAFF WAGES			
Staff Manager & Staff	47	50	52
Front of House:	44	44	44
including Director's Secretary, Business Manager, Box Office, Cleaners, Linkman, Programme-sellers, Cloakrooms, Caretaker etc.			

LIGHT & HEAT	15	18	18
SCENERY (average per play)	30	30	30
PROPERTIES & COSTUMES (hire or making)	10	15	15
SUNDRY Printing, Posters etc., Programmes, Books & Parts, Stationery, Telephone, Postages, Maintenance & Cleaning	10	15	15
ACCOUNTANTS	2	3	3
	£365	£467	£519

If a flop were taken off during its second week there could be a saving, but even so some £200 of costs would continue while a new production was hurried forward.

The steep rise in costs with a successful play is explained by the percentage principle applying for author's royalties and for artistes' salaries, both of which were entirely just and fair. The case of the salaries of artistes is one that has been misrepresented. In the first experimental months there was general acceptance of £4 or £5 per week but with the growing success of the theatre there had to be adjustments. For a time salaries from £5 to £10 were paid. Then I introduced a sliding-scale arrangement for the more important parts in a play. These were graded up to £10, £12 and £15 per week. It is important to note that the salary offered was always based on the importance of the part and not on the artiste's name or status. Later still, in the case of leading parts on which the success of a play depended, a percentage on House-receipts above the 'get-out' figure of, say, £325 was occasionally paid on top of the basic £15; the total salary thus paid might come to nearer £30. In one case, in an emergency, it reached £45. This explains how the artistes' salary list might rise to over £200. It also explains how I was able to hold together a company of the acting standard evidenced by the cast lists. Artistes might be offered, and quite frequently were offered, West-End salaries of over £50 to £75 by commercial managers after some particular success at Hampstead, but loyally preferred to remain with the Everyman company.

One factor that artistes found attractive was the permanency of their engagement. A salary of £15 per week over a long period was more satisfactory than sporadic employment in the West End. At the Everyman the company rehearsed one play during the day while performing another at night and so there was always a weekly pay envelope. It was a boast of the Everyman that it was the first London theatre to adopt the terms of engagement-contracts that were being sought for the acting profession. At the date of opening the 'Valentine Contract' was in force. Then, after a struggle with the commercial managements an improved contract was settled by the Actors' Association. This in turn was replaced by another negotiated by Equity. The current form was immediately adopted at the Everyman; not that many contracts were actually signed because artistes knew that the minimum terms and conditions would be observed and there was mutual trust.

Advertising was a heavy and non-variable item but our allocation was never adequate. The coverage for London is enormous. On one occasion I protested to the London Omnibus Company that, although I was paying for 100 positions on the outside of buses, I had stood for half an hour in Piccadilly to see one of my posters and not one had passed me. They sent a courteous reply enclosing a list of 100 buses with their numbers and routes on which our poster was displayed. As to Tubes, it seemed one might travel all day on a criss-cross of routes and see no more than two or three posters.

The smallest space in the Theatre Announcement Columns was all we could afford and that in only a selection of the leading papers. This was taken as a grievance by some, and the Advertising Manager of one of the leading 'Sundays' telephoned to protest. After I had explained the limited amount of cash we could spend he snapped, "All right. . . . No advertisement; No notices". In London even regular supporters expect to pick up a daily or evening paper to find what play is on and details about it. For helpful publicity, accordingly, we were dependent on good notices by the critics and the columnists' write-ups of first-night audiences, stage-clothes, amusing or catastrophic happenings on which they could hang a story. Very helpful they were and would telephone often to ask for anything that they could use.

The foyer coffee bar, in spite of the refusal of a Licence, made a useful profit, which fluctuated with the success of plays between

£15 and 15s. The bookstall, stocked with a wide selection of plays and books, magazines with articles and illustrations of the Continental and American 'New Movement' was run by a young actress from the company, Dodie Smith, who later wrote the highly successful play *Autumn Crocus* and followed that with other successes.

One most important aim of the Everyman was to encourage a revival in English play-writing. It was a serious disappointment that so few of the plays submitted reached a standard, in matter or writing, that made them worthy of production. But some other managers held different opinions about acceptability, and with the growing repute of the Everyman there was much pressure for opportunities to stage their choices. So not to bar such experiment by others, temporary 'lets' were occasionally made. In every case a lump sum or a Guarantee was received of an amount to cover standing costs. While it must be admitted that these were sometimes very useful in providing breathing space to bring forward a production of our own and to cover the loss if the theatre had been closed, they did not add to the repute of the theatre. In the long view they were a mistake in policy. Our own experiments with new dramatists showed that audiences did not take readily to new author try-outs. The paucity of interesting new writing for the theatre in the 1920's is in marked contrast to the level and the amount of such work in the years following the second world war.

Another main cause of small audiences was the location. Over this both Shaw and Galsworthy proved wrong in their belief that Hampstead would provide a regular nucleus of supporters. *The Manchester Guardian* wrote in its January 1922 review of the year's drama in London:

"The Management of this little theatre has vastly improved in punctuality and timing of its Plays; the acting has always been excellent. But Mr. MacDermott had to fight geography as well as public poverty and the neglect of good drama. Except for those who live in the immediate neighbourhood, or close to the stations on the Hampstead Tube, the journey is a tedious discouragement. For people in Kensington or Chelsea a visit to the Everyman is a considerable excursion. Distance lends no enchantment on a cold or foggy night."

Lastly there was the perennial difficulty of rent for the building. The conversion of the Drill Hall into the attractive theatre was paid for out of the funds subscribed for working capital. The Leases of the theatre and also of the old Fire Station were held by Mr. Frank Foster. The completed theatre and workshop was let to the original Everyman Theatres Ltd. at a weekly rental of £10. He was also one of the supporters who from time to time made large donations to the working deficits, mostly to meet artistes' salaries when a play failed. At the end of the disappointing International Season, when his large donation had been absorbed, he intimated that he could no longer continue to provide further money and he withdrew entirely from direct association with the theatre in December 1922 and let the premises to me at the same rental of £10 per week.

1922 proved to be a year of comparative ease by reason of the success of the Shaw productions. In 1923 came the first real financial success with the transfer of *At Mrs. Beam's* to the Royalty Theatre and an exhilarating inflow of weekly profit that lasted until nearly the end of the year. These substantial winnings were all paid into the Everyman account and used to clear off the accumulated trading debts that remained after the old company was wound-up. At last the theatre project seemed set-fair. But the success also brought a surprise pressure to increase the rent: Mr. Foster explained that he was faced with a new policy in business and he wished to recover some of the money he had contributed to the Everyman. He contended that as profits were being made from the Royalty I could afford to pay more for the Everyman. The rent was increased by £10 per week and by an additional £10, following the other successful transfers in 1924. I protested strongly but the alternative was the termination of tenancy.

The rent then stood at £30 per week. Successes like *Home Affairs* in February, 1925, suggested that there would be hope of survival, but the anticipated transfer did not take place. Towards the end of the year the final confrontation with Mr. Foster followed the receipt of the usual telegram: "Meet me at King's Cross Refreshment Room to-night". The ultimatum was payment of all arrears and an increase of rent by way of a 5 per cent of House Receipts over £300 weekly. I gambled with a production of the stage version of the best-seller novel *Sweet Pepper*; and lost.

Earlier I had announced *The Man who was Thursday* and I now tackled it as my 'swan-song'. It was a gratifying success and as a production received some of the critics' best notices. The audiences grew steadily and I remain convinced that it could have had a long run in the West End given time to negotiate the transfer, but during rehearsals I had received final notice to quit on the last day of January, 1926, and was in no position to negotiate.

My tenure of my Everyman was at an end.

Envoi

Sometimes when in London I have gone up to the Everyman Cinema, and, kindly received by its Manager, been put into my old D.D.'s seat in the back corner. As the lights fade for the film, I sense movement, hear voices, see ghosts.

Ellen Terry, still lovely and gracious, peering through enormous spectacles to find her cues. . . .

Athene Seyler, supposedly murdered, mincing down three steps to attend her own funeral service. . . .

Felix Aylmer, as Cusins in Major Barbara, dry like a Fino Sherry. . . .

Edith Evans, exquisitely gowned and looking supremely beautiful in one of her richest performances. . . .

Jean Cadell as Miss Shoe, with Raymond Massey—head buried in a huge gramophone horn—snapping at her "And I'll bet none of your valves work either" . . .

Claude Rains as Napoleon, marking positions on his war-map with chewed grape-skins . . . and again, his rich voice almost breathless as the dying Dubedat. . . .

Bernard Shaw suddenly leaping up at rehearsal, dashing down to the stage exclaiming in his most Dublinesque "No . . . no . . . not like that at ahl!"

G.K.C.'s enormous bulk struggling to heave himself out of his double stall still belly-laughing at his own play. . . .

The close of *Twelfth Night*, opalescent colour against sunny white walls, with Isabel Jeans in a honey-gold wig, and Harold Scott gently singing "A great while ago the world began . . ."

I hear the echo from Lear

> "He that has and a little tiny wit
> Must make content with his fortunes fit"

and I am duly humbled.

> To all these Ghosts, and many mo'
> Hail! . . . and Farewell.

Kilmartin 1964
Port Appin, Argyll 1974
(Where the rain it raineth every day)

Cast Lists and Critics

A selection of ten Everyman productions has been made from Mr. MacDermott's collection of programmes and press-cuttings, not entirely at random but with some design to show the quality and imagination that often prevailed in the casting.

The specimen extracts from reviews have been chosen with rather more forethought, to comment on the production and acting rather than on the merits of the play. They are in no way exhaustive but give some idea of the production standards, frequently novel at the time, and the achievements of the Everyman viewed in the contemporary theatre scene.

Here are reactions to two Shakespearean productions, showing a difference of opinion between those who could lament a break with tradition and others who caught the point of fresh interpretation. Here are comments on two Shaw revivals; the first impression of O'Neill on London audiences; the impact of the young Coward; and a clutch of notices of an early triumph of Edith Evans which still echo their concerted recognition.

The complete collection of programmes, press-cutting books, photographs, production diaries, management announcements and other material will be available for reference in the archive deposited with the Theatre Museum when it opens in Somerset House.

ROMEO AND JULIET (18.11.20)

Chorus	DOROTHY MASSINGHAM	*Escalus*	W. EDWARD STIRLING
Sampson	CHARLES MARFORD	*Romeo*	NICHOLAS HANNEN
Gregory	MICHAEL RAGHAN	*Paris*	JOHN GARSIDE
Abraham	RUSSELL SEDGWICK	*Peter*	HAROLD SCOTT
Balthasar	CHARLES KOOP	*Nurse*	AGNES THOMAS
Benvolio	DOUGLAS JEFFERIES	*Juliet*	MURIEL PRATT
Tybalt	HENRY OSCAR	*Mercutio*	LAURENCE HANRAY
Capulet	REGINALD RIVINGTON	*An Old Man*	ROLAND GRANT
Lady Capulet	MARGARET CARTER	*Friar Laurence*	BREMBER WILLS
Montague	FRANK AINSLIE	*An Apothecary*	HAROLD SCOTT
Lady Montague	EDITH HARLEY	*Friar John*	MICHAEL RAGHAN

Ladies and Gentlemen, Pages, Watchmen, Attendants, etc.:

HAZEL JONES, LOIS HEATHERLEY, AUDREY CAMERON, M. STEWART, HILDA MAUDE, FRANCES PHAIR, ELLEN POLLAK and others

The victim of untoward circumstances on the first night of its performance, Mr. Norman MacDermott's revival of *Romeo and Juliet* has now been brought to the state of perfection originally aimed at by the producer. The wisdom of presenting the piece in twenty-one scenes and almost in its entirety is still, however, a point open to debate . . . shortcomings apart, Mr. MacDermott may justly be congratulated on a production faithfully reflecting the spirit and the significance of Shakespeare's work. Approaching his task with a perfectly open mind and a complete disregard of tradition, he has even dared to discard the farcical business between the Nurse and Peter which custom and long service have so mistakenly sanctified. The scenery is simple, but, save the balcony set, quite·effective, and the costumes highly picturesque. In Miss Muriel Pratt, moreover, he has found a Juliet of talent and unusual sensibility. In appearance, happily, she is sufficiently youthful to justify the poet's description of his heroine. The opening duet was played by her with exquisite tenderness and girlish feeling . . . as the piece progressed it quickly became evident that Miss Pratt had a fund of emotional force upon which to draw . . . an emotional strength surprising in so youthful an actress. From the culminating test of the potion scene Miss Pratt also emerged triumphantly. Without the slightest suspicion of ranting, hardly, indeed, raising her voice above a whisper, she succeeded in giving full expression to the horror born of the fearful picture painted by her own fancy.

Besides her Juliet Mr. Nicholas Hannen's Romeo seemed just a little lacking in colour. His love scenes were very tenderly played and his lines spoken clearly and with appropriate emphasis. What one missed was that final touch of the artist's imagination which lifts a performance on to a really high level.   *Daily Telegraph*, 1 December, 1920

There is a theatre in London where in a performance lasting just over three hours twenty changes of scenery are made, each of which, on an average, takes less than three-quarters of a minute to effect. This feat is accomplished nightly at the Everyman Theatre, Hampstead, in the play *Romeo and Juliet*. Mr. Norman MacDermott, the director, explained how it is done. The scenery used is his own invention, and is constructed on entirely new lines. It is made up of columns and arches which remain in position throughout the evening; fixed to them are panels 20 feet high by 3 feet across, which are on hinges. To change the scene the panels are merely turned over like the pages of a book, and the stage lighting altered. *Evening News*, 2 December, 1920

Since the first night *Romeo and Juliet* has run so smoothly that only some six minutes have been necessary for changing all the scenes. Little as that seems, I think it is too much for an ideal performance of Shakespeare. . . . *Daily News*, 4 December, 1920

THE SHEWING-UP OF BLANCO POSNET (14.3.21)

Babsy	MARJORIE GABAIN	*Sheriff Kemp*	FELIX AYLMER
Lottie	HELEN BOYCE	*Feemy Evans*	MURIEL PRATT
Hannah	EDITH HARLEY	*The Foreman of the Jury*	
Jessie	MIMOSA VALENTINE		GEORGE HAYES
Emma	AUDREY CAMERON	*Nestor*	DOUGLAS JEFFERIES
Elder Daniels	HAROLD SCOTT	*Squinty*	IRENE DARRELL
Blanco Posnet	BREMBER WILLS	*Waggoner Jo*	ROBERT CRAIG
Strapper Kemp	LESLIE J. BANKS	*The Woman*	HAZEL JONES

Women and Cowboys: G. JOHNSTONE-CAMPBELL, FABIA DRAKE,
IVY BELL, FRANCES PHAIR, LILIAN TAYLOR and others

The triple bill of Shaw plays just inaugurated at the little Hampstead Repertory Theatre is chiefly of interest because in it *The Shewing-up of Blanco Posnet* is included for its first really public performance in England. It has been produced privately several times, but not until now have you been able to pay your money and walk in to see it. . . . Our stage is distinctly the better for being able to add this little play to its store of material, and the Everyman Theatre will add greatly to its laurels by its presentation. Blanco Posnet is a fine stage character, full of unexpected twists which convince you at the same time as they surprise you. It gives Mr. Brember Wills the opportunity for an unforgettable piece of acting, full of colour as crude and as powerful as Mr. Shaw's writing. It is a really outstanding achievement, strong, spirited, humorous and sincere. Miss Muriel Pratt flings herself into the part of the disgraceful Feemy with appropriate abandon. . . . Mr. Felix Aylmer is about as near perfect in the part of the sheriff as a man well can be. . . . The crowds are well handled and the play well produced.
Daily Telegraph, 15 March, 1921

The Everyman Theatre gave it every chance to appear at its best, and are much to be congratulated on their production. In the part of the Sheriff Mr. Felix Aylmer was perfect. He does not have to rant nor to portray delirium tremens, as do one or two of the other characters, but the rough incisiveness with which he controlled the trial and the brutal joviality of his concluding remarks were all part of an admirable study. . . . *Manchester Guardian*, 15 March, 1921

The Shewing-up of Blanco Posnet . . . is not only the best-acted play that has been done in this theatre, but is also the best-produced. Moreover, this performance of *Blanco Posnet* is much the best that I have seen. . . . The Blanco of Mr. Brember Wills was extraordinarily good, giving what I have never seen given to Blanco before, a sense of nervous apprehension at the mysterious acts of God. Miss Muriel Pratt, as Feemy Evans, played better than I have ever seen her act before. . . . This was a first-rate production in every respect, and I am glad to see that it is finding its reward. . . . *The Observer*, 20 March, 1921

There is something superbly ironical about the combination of Shaw and Hampstead. I am seized with laughter as I think about it. But, at any rate, Shaw has brought prosperity in full and overflowing measure to the little Everyman Theatre supervised by Mr. Norman MacDermott. Every performance is sold out, and you must book your seats beforehand. . . . I have not the least doubt that this play alone will fill the little Everyman Theatre for months to come. It needs no push from me. *Sunday Times*, 20 March, 1921

MAN AND SUPERMAN (23.5.21)

Roebuck Ramsden		*Ann Whitefield*	MURIEL PRATT
	DOUGLAS JEFFERIES	*Miss Ramsden*	EDITH HARLEY
The Parlormaid		*Violet Robinson*	HAZEL JONES
	MIMOSA VALENTINE	*Straker*	BREMBER WILLS
Octavius Robinson		*Hector Malone, Junr.*	
	WILLIAM ARMSTRONG		FELIX AYLMER
John Tanner	NICHOLAS HANNEN	*Hector Malone, Senr.*	
Mrs. Whitefield			JOSEPH DODD
	MARGARET CARTER		

At the end of his extremely successful Shaw season Mr. Norman MacDermott can produce *Man and Superman* with the triumphant gesture of a bridge player who takes the last trick with the ace of trumps. This is about the most brilliant of all Mr. Shaw's plays, and would need to be extraordinarily badly acted in order to fail to attract. Badly acted it certainly is not . . . altogether, when a few performances have smoothed out some of the creases, this will be as good a performance as the Hampstead company has to its credit. *Daily Telegraph*, 24 May, 1921

Bernard Shaw was present last night at the Everyman Theatre, Hampstead, at the revival of his *Man and Superman*. He must have been much gratified at the excellence of the performance, which was as near perfection as one could expect. . . . The Everyman company did wonders. Nicholas Hannen (made up with a red early-Shavian beard) was an earnest and virile John Tanner, and Muriel Pratt was excellent as the designing Ann. . . . This is certainly one of the best achievements of Mr. MacDermott's Shaw season at Hampstead.

Star, 24 May, 1921

This week's revival is finely played, and produced with that economy of effect which stamps the art of Norman MacDermott. You should see how the simplest cream-coloured arcade, a luminous sky, and a balcony, the whole drenched in a hot orange light, gives the perfect Spanish atmosphere for the villa courtyard in Act III. At the ******** we should have had a dreadful multiplication of Moorish filigree and "real Palms" to distract the eye and obfuscate the reason. Felix Aylmer and Joseph Dodd are a sheer joy as the two Americans, and Nicholas Hannen a sufficiently Shavian John Tanner. I thought Muriel Pratt's Ann Whitefield was a little on the vicious side, but as the Sage never stopped beaming and chuckling, I take it he approved of this reading. Altogether the Everyman company are giving some of the most polished acting in London. While intelligent comedy flourishes on the Hampstead peaks one need not regret the languishing (so to speak) of lingerie in the valley.

Daily Express, 25 May, 1921

IN THE ZONE (15.6.21)

Smitty	BREMBER WILLS	*Scotty*	WILLIAM ARMSTRONG
Davis	JOSEPH DODD	*Jack*	NICHOLAS HANNEN
Swanson	GEORGE CARR	*Driscoll*	FELIX AYLMER
Ivan	DOUGLAS JEFFERIES	*Cocky*	HAROLD SCOTT

Mr. MacDermott's interesting *Pedlar's Basket* contains a one-act play which alone is enough to give it distinction. This is *In the Zone* by Eugene O'Neill, the American author of various pieces promised to us but not yet produced in London. It is not a perfect one-act play. . . . But Mr. O'Neill is a dramatist. . . . His may prove to be one of the foremost talents of the stage, and it is note-worthy that he makes his bow to England in our least fashionable but most hopeful playhouse. I find it tiresome that the merits of this play . . . should inevitably be discussed in the same breath as the propriety of its language. But there it is: the Lord Chamberlain's Department has lost its sense of humour again. . . . Here Mr. Brember Wills, the most temperamental player of the Everyman company, seizes the imagination by five minutes of nervous acting of the highest order. . . .

Illustrated Sporting and Dramatic News, 25 June, 1921

In the Zone . . . it was interesting to see it as a matter of curiosity, for Mr. O'Neill is the author of *Emperor Jones*, the play in which the negro tragedian Gilpin has made a deep impression on New York, and it supports the stories which people who have seen the longer play tell of a rich imagination that is at work on new and untraditional material. It is a picture of fear. . . . It is exciting and impressive and, in the way it sounds a note not in the gamut of contemporary drama, extremely hopeful. One is grateful to Mr. Norman MacDermott for giving one the chance to see it, and for producing such a piece of concerted acting; each sailor had his own individuality ,and they worked together magnificently in creating the sense of increasing fear.

Time and Tide, 24 June, 1921. Miss Rebecca West

The Everyman Theatre, Hampstead, is, at the moment, the most vital dramatic enterprise in London. It seems to have the most energetic actors, and certainly the most alert audiences; it continues to attract, even if it has not yet succeeded in satisfying. . . . On the whole it is an interesting show. It reveals the fact that Mr. MacDermott is an artist who has not quite found himself, but will be a force to reckon with when he does. We have had, and have, all sorts of attempts to restore the art of drama, and I fancy they are coming to a focus at the Everyman. The whole mood of the place is different from that of any other theatre known to me; it is alive, and its very crudities (like Mr. MacDermott's tilting at the Censor) are the crudities of young blood. *The Pedlar's Basket* more than once perilously came near to beauty—although the miracle did not quite happen. But we expect it to happen at the Everyman. *New Age*, 29 June, 1921. John Francis Hope

In the Zone provided the best piece of concerted acting that the Everyman company has yet shown us . . . an admirably written play, perfectly acted. *The Observer*, 19 June, 1921

MARY STUART (25.9.22)

John Hunter	RICHARD BIRD	*Darnley*	HARCOURT WILLIAMS
Andrew Boyd	H. O. NICHOLSON	*Thomas Randolph*	
Mary Stuart	LAURA COWIE		DOUGLAS JEFFERIES
Mary Beaton	CLAIRE HARRIS	*Bothwell*	RANDLE AYRTON
David Riccio	HAROLD SCOTT		

. . . Thus once more has Mr. Drinkwater gone to the suburbs for his first hearing, though there is little doubt that, had he so desired, he would have had no great difficulty in securing a West-End theatre for the production. *Birmingham Mail*, 26 September, 1922

In the present case, Mr. Drinkwater is very fortunate to have Miss Laura Cowie to play the Queen. Her acting as Mary is interesting even more than it is moving, as it is intellectual rather than emotional. This is not to say that Miss Cowie fails to suggest the deep passion of Mary—deep calling vainly to deep; all this she does. But Mary throughout the play is dissecting motives, calculating odds, weighing hopes and fears; she is acting not under the blind impulse of her passion, but in accordance with (or in spite of) her reason. It is on this side of the character that Miss Cowie's work is specially distinguished. It is a performance which enhances her already high reputation for delicate work. . . .

Daily Telegraph, 26 September, 1922

. . . The best performance after Miss Cowie's was an old man of our time, Andrew Boyd, by Mr. H. O. Nicholson, who with nothing but talking to do talked with a conviction of character, lovable and understanding. *Birmingham Post*, 26 September, 1922

. . . The whole evening was a triumph of production, and for Miss Laura Cowie in particular, who most valiantly made bricks without straw. She was so beautiful, so graceful in every gesture, so dignified to the tips of her fingers, that I felt there was no part that she could not adorn. Mr. Scott, too, gave a first-rate performance of Riccio, and Mr. Harcourt Williams was excellent as Darnley. . . . In fact, the production made me feel optimistic, not only about the Everyman Theatre, but about the English stage.

New Statesman, 30 September, 1922. Francis Birrell

At the end, Mr. Drinkwater, in reply to an insistent call, made a speech. He told a story, however, about Hampstead that suggested to the Hampstead people that his ideas about Hampstead were less sound than about Mary Queen of Scots. A friend of his that day had tried to buy coffee cups but found that they were too large. The shopkeeper had explained that "People in Hampstead don't drink black coffee". The silence for a moment was such that you might have heard a cup of black coffee drop. It was hard to have the only theatre in London without a gallery, and yet to have it said that you don't drink black coffee. A bold man, Mr. Drinkwater. *Manchester Guardian*, 26 September, 1922

TWELFTH NIGHT (22.12.22)

Orsino, Duke of Ilyria		*Feste*	HAROLD SCOTT
	BALIOL HOLLOWAY	*Olivia*	ISABEL JEANS
Curio	WILLIAM MONK	*Malvolio*	HERBERT WARING
Valentine	RICHARD BIRD	*Fabian*	RAYMOND MASSEY
Viola	MARY BARTON	*Sebastian*	ION SWINLEY
A Sea Captain		*Antonio*	SETON BLACKDEN
	DOUGLAS JEFFERIES	*1st Officer*	HUGH WILLIAMS
Sir Toby Belch	FRANK CELLIER	*2nd Officer*	THURLOW FINN
Maria	MARGARET YARDE	*Priest*	DOUGLAS JEFFERIES
Sir Andrew Aguecheek		*1st Page*	JOYCE FAGAN
	FRED O'DONOVAN	*2nd Page*	PRIMROSE MORGAN

Mr. Norman MacDermott has designed a new setting. . . . The scheme makes possible several neat stage-groupings. . . . But the set hardly does all the programme claims for it. Its unrelieved Oriental whiteness is tiring to the eyes, and one misses the Box Hedge scene, in which Sir Toby and Sir Andrew make sport of Malvolio when he finds the fake letter. As it is, the Knights and Fabian are stowed away forward on the extreme edges of a narrow apron-stage.

Morning Post, 23 December, 1922

Yet it is the essence of the play that there need be no contradiction of one mood by the other. . . . Why, then, the lack of harmony . . . ? . . . for our part, we believe the fault lay in the producer's quest of the unusual, the sudden blackenings of the stage, and the thrusting forward of the watchers in the letter scene. *The Times*, 23 December, 1922

The first thing I want to say about the Everyman production of *Twelfth Night* is that it is the best Shakespearean revival I have ever seen in London. Naturally it is not perfect. It would be easy enough to pick holes in the delicate fabric and then return it with a superior sniff. But such a procedure would be not only easy, but criminal and imbecile; for visitors to the Everyman Theatre will see the play intelligently and respectfully produced. The beautiful and simple *décor*, the appropriate and sympathetic dresses are equidistant both from a cardboard naturalism and from the trickiness of *art nouveau*: the stage is based on a happy compromise between the Shakespearean bare boards and modern science, with the result that the play can be given word for word in about two and a half hours. It is acted by people who realise that the heritage of our English tongue is a possession worth the keeping, and that Shakespeare is more important than the tricks of the stage. Thus they can reconstruct for us Shakespeare's romantic unearthly-human paradise. . . . Orsino, Sebastion and Viola spoke their lines with a sensitiveness rarely heard on the English stage. . . . I thought Mr. Herbert Waring's Malvolio excellent. It was a bright idea to get him up as our intolerable and incomparable James; but above all, he avoided the vice of sentimentalising Malvolio until he becomes the hero of the play. . . . But, O Margaret Yarde, most adorable of women, what words of mine can adequately praise thee? After a long succession of pretty giggling Marias, snatched from the beauty chorus of some musical comedy, what a joy was it to see thee sweep on in thy broad Shakespearean humanity, thy unquenchable gusto, thy opulent grace! But the production aimed at and achieved a higher ideal than the providing of star-turns for intelligent actors and actresses. One and all gladly fitted themselves into the framework of the piece. . . . There was at any rate one member of the first-night audience who felt that a new chapter had been opened in the history of the English stage; that the long Victorian night is over, and the sky is radiant with a better dawn.

New Statesman, 30 December, 1922. Francis Birrell

THE VORTEX (25.11.24)

Preston	CLAIRE KEEP	*Tom Veryan*	ALAN HOLLIS
Helen Saville	MARY ROBSON	*Nicky Lancaster*	NOEL COWARD
Pauncefort Quentin		*David Lancaster*	
	F. KINSEY PEILE		BROMLEY DAVENPORT
Clara Hibbert	MILLIE SIM	*Bunty Mainwaring*	MOLLY KERR
Florence Lancaster		*Bruce Fairlight*	IVOR BARNARD
	LILIAN BRAITHWAITE		

His play is a study of rottenness, of extravagant misery among extravagant pleasures, of restlessness and unbridled impulse, of "nerve". It is a study that has wit, observation, and a sincerity, leaping out between flippances, which is its peculiar merit. . . .
The Times, 26 November, 1924

At the close of the first act . . . it seemed that the author had determined to go one better than *Our Betters*. Here were the same segments of the same vicious circle . . . tiresome company unless your author happens to be a Congreve at the top of his form and his genius runs to a prose symphony of cynicism. Mr. Coward is clever, but not so witty that we could have relished two more acts of his fops and libertines. . . . Then suddenly and fortunately he changes his tune. Young Nicky Lancaster, played by the author himself, has come back from studying music in Paris. . . . The play becomes genuinely and deeply interesting the moment that feeling comes in and the dramatic conflict surges up between the boy's decent instinct and his villainous environment . . . the boy's character becomes a thing of penetration, and his nervous fumblings at the door of rebellion are written and acted by Mr. Coward in a way that drives at the root of reality. Miss Lilian Braithwaite carries the mother's part from the shallows of complacent lechery to the depths of self-realisation with an artistry that makes no mistake in any of the changing emotional levels.
Manchester Guardian, 26 November, 1924

. . . There is a situation at the end of the second act which has the touch of genius, and the dénouement is of genuine power. But it introduces us to a crowd of people whom we can only describe as diseased . . . there is a touch of genius here. We can remember nothing quite like it in all our experience of the theatre. But its power is of a diseased kind. It has the Beardsley touch. *Daily Telegraph*, 27 November, 1924

. . . He takes his place as a writer whose work has to be seriously taken into account . . . the play is one which will not die easily, and is safe to achieve success at any West-End theatre. . . . There is more than enough to compensate for what is wrong with this play. It is a better (though worse constructed) play than *Our Betters* in the same genre. *Our Betters* is a caricature. *The Vortex* wrings our own withers. It holds up the mirror to 1924. *Daily Graphic*, 29 November, 1924. S. P. B. Mais

THE PAINTED SWAN (16.3.25)

Thompson	HAROLD B. MEADE	*Philip Jordon*	ALLAN JEAYES
Lord William Cathcart		*Lady Emily Cathcart*	
	FELIX AYLMER		MARGARET CARTER
Selina	ELISSA LANDI	*Anny (Lady Candover)*	
Mrs. Martineau	MURIEL POPE		EDITH EVANS
Mr. Molyneux		*Ninian (Lord Candover)*	
	CLIFFORD MOLLISON		FRANK CELLIER
Timothy Carstairs	ROBERT HARRIS		

Or should it not rather be called Miss Edith Evans's play? It is at once the merit and the good fortune of *The Painted Swan*, produced at the Everyman Theatre tonight, that Princess Bibesco provides Miss Evans with a scene in which the sheer hammering power of her tragical gift had the fullest chance to beat out a noble pattern of distress. It is one of those scenes of discovery which began when tragedy was born. . . . Miss Evans made the old grief seem new with a fresh-found anguish; as her illusion was rent and the curtain parted to reveal reality the scene was as dreadful as though a child were in quenchless pain. It was great acting to grace an occasion hardly of its stature. . . . In any case the depth of the illusion was in this instance justified by the depth of the consequent disaster, coupled with the amazing power of Miss Evans to make a heart crack publicly. . . . In the firing party Mr. Clifford Mollison and Mr. Felix Aylmer made the best of the ammunition. Mr. Frank Cellier and Mr. Allan Jeayes were admirable as Candover and Jordon. But *The Painted Swan* is a play of one scene and one player. Miss Edith Evans, a little too nervously mannered in her first two acts, was irresistible in the third, where emotion could have a full theatrical release. *Manchester Guardian*, 17 March, 1925

. . . Mr. Felix Aylmer's wise sententiousness and Miss Muriel Pope's feline brilliance enables these two players to stand out from the rest of the background. As Ann, Miss Edith Evans makes you feel she is doing wonders with a part in which she does not quite believe. As her lover, Mr. Allan Jeayes bounds to unimaginable heights, and succeeds perfectly in getting his effects—though he makes Ann's love for Mr. Jordon a little hard to swallow. As her husband, Mr. Frank Cellier is a perfect miracle of pompous self-sufficiency. *Daily Telegraph*, 17 March, 1925

In the part of Ann Miss Edith Evans gave one of those exquisite performances which strengthens the arm and convictions of those who set her down as a comedienne of the highest accomplishment. Not a shade of subtlety escaped her throughout the whole piece, nor—and this was more important—did she fail to convey that exact shade to us. She made of Ann a gracious, lonely soul, sufficient to herself as a flower is sufficient to itself—or we presume so—until her unguarded senses led her astray. . . . Her determined refusal to see the grossness in Jordon was full of beauty, and the mingled horror and tragedy of the ultimate revelation were very finely done.

Sunday Times, 22 March, 1925. James Agate

Fortunately her play has a brilliant cast; fortunately it has Miss Edith Evans to portray her central figure; fortunately also the third act gives Miss Evans a chance to exercise her sweeping tragic power. . . . Miss Evans plays her part with a nervous intensity and a revelation of a romantic woman's disillusion that fairly tears the play out of its gawdy trimmings and makes it as actual as life itself. . . . Miss Evans gradually dominates the trivial scene and shed over it the sovereignty of her portraiture. *Saturday Review*, 21 March, 1925

THE WILD DUCK (30.6.25)

Petterson	J. HUBERT LESLIE	*Werle*	GEORGE MERRITT
Old Ekdal	BREMBER WILLS	*Gregers Werle*	ION SWINLEY
Mrs. Sorby	MARY ROBSON	*Hjalmar*	MILTON ROSMER
Councillor Flor		*Gina Ekdal*	SYBIL ARUNDALE
	CHARLES A. STAITE	*Hedvig*	ANGELA BADDELEY
Councillor Balle	HAROLD SCOTT	*Dr. Relling*	SYDNEY BLAND
Councillor Kaspersen		*Molvik*	HAROLD SCOTT
	VICTOR H. LESLIE		

A performance, then, which at once preserves the coherence of the wild-duck symbolism and avoids the damage of which it might so easily be made the cause, is a general achievement of the whole cast. Last night we found that the play was so consistently performed that the conflict—for conflict it is—between Ibsen at his best and Ibsen led astray was very little apparent. Miss Arundale as Gina, acted with a quiet firmness and strength; Mr. Swinley's Gregers Werle was remarkable in truth and smoothness of development; Mr. Milton Rosmer gave a very brilliant performance as Hjalmar; and Miss Angela Baddeley was a beautiful and moving Hedwig—a child to whom an older wisdom was continually and secretly hinting. It was an evening of real distinction. *The Times*, 1 July, 1925

The result is a rendering rare and refreshing indeed. We have never seen a more admirable Gregers than Mr. Swinley's, a more varied and buoyant and self-pitying Hjalmar than Mr. Rosmer's, or a more solid and life-like elder Werle than Mr. George Merritt's. . . . Nor can anything but congratulation be extended to Miss Angela Baddeley for as touching a rendering of the character of the girl Hedvig as the London stage can have seen since Miss Winifred Fraser played the part years ago and became famous in a night. *Daily Telegraph*, 1 July, 1925

There are those who will decide that they had better go to *The Wild Duck* while it is being played at the Everyman Theatre in the half-humorous spirit in which they visit a museum, but they must be warned that *The Wild Duck* is still something more than a museum piece . . . and it has not been regarded as one by the producers. It is perhaps the best cast play now to be seen in London, and this though it was seldom seen, even during the Ibsen craze, because its casting is so difficult. There was always the problem of the little Hedwig. . . . She has been found at last in Miss Angela Baddeley, who acted like a little angel and looked like a Greuze.   *Evening Standard*, 1 July, 1925

The Everyman Theatre production of *The Wild Duck* is not to be missed by any Londoner with an interest in the theatre. It was a useful shock to go to the theatre piously, as to a museum, and then to find the play full of the Pirandellism we were feeling so modern about last week. The acting and production are almost above criticism. . . .
The Queen, 8 July, 1925

Miss Sybil Arundale has won favour in various kinds of plays, mostly musical, but that she should venture on Ibsen seems daring . . . at Hampstead the play is acted just as ordinary plays are, and not in the awestruck fashion that one has known sometimes adopted with Ibsen, and the revival should be all the more popular on that account.
Morning Post, 3 July, 1925

THE MAN WHO WAS THURSDAY (20.1.26)

Lucien Gregory	*Sunday (the President)* ROY BYFORD
DOUGLAS BURBIDGE	*Tuesday* ALEXANDER FIELD
Gabriel Syme (Thursday)	*Wednesday (the Marquis)*
CAMPBELL GULLAN	GUY LE FEUVRE
Rosamund Gregory	*Friday (the Professor)*
JOSEPHINE WILSON	STANLEY LATHBURY
Comrade Buttons DAN F. ROE	*Saturday (the Doctor)*
Monday (the Secretary)	CHARLES BENNETT
EARLE GREY	*A Barmaid* UNA O'CONNOR
A Waiter VINCENT BREIT	*Usher* GERALD JEROME

Anarchists: V. BREIT, A. DODDINGTON, P. GOODYER, R. GRAHAM, P. HUNTER, G. JEROME, M. JOHNS, C. LANDEAU, V. H. LESLIE, F. LEWIS

You may complain that in the matter of the camouflaged policeman the gaff is blown too soon and that the succession of similar revelations grows tedious, or than people do not behave like this, or that you should not carry on lengthy conversations entirely by *non sequiturs.* . . . But equally you may take the contrary view and hold that the author's genius is a shining star reserved by Mr. MacDermott for his setting.

But whichever opinion you hold you will not, I think, deny enjoyment of an evening which contains so much pure fun. That the fun is often irrelevant is an objection of little account. . . . The piece is extremely well acted by a company whose names it is a pleasure to write down. . . . The impressionist production was as stimulating as anything I have seen in a London theatre. . . .

Sunday Times, 24 January, 1926. James Agate

For one act of *The Man who was Thursday* on the first night I sat next to Mr. Chesterton, who paid a tribute to the actors by a great many irresistible laughs. He said in his speech afterwards that although he had not written the play, but only the book, he felt a little uncomfortable about the question of applause or appreciation. He felt it might be met by clapping with one hand, but it didn't work. Neither could he laugh only at the phrases he hadn't written, because it was at the acting he was laughing. Altogether he was in very good form.

Daily Mirror, 22 January, 1974

Five and a half years is a longer time than I remembered it. In five and a half years, then, we have journeyed to Hampstead as critics, say something like once or twice a month, the summer months not excepted. In the early days we have waited for the half-hour-late rise of the Everyman curtain, and many times in five and a half years waited, watch in hand, for the Everyman curtain's fall, with Fleet Street before midnight becoming an ever-remoter possibility. In these material respects the Everyman has sometimes known how to make itself the critic's hell. But I have no intention of forgetting also that in every year of the five-and-a-half it has produced incomparably more good plays than any other single London theatre. Or that Mr. MacDermott's successors will be lucky if they do as well. *Evening Standard*, 21 January, 1926

Mr. MacDermott must have ploughed through some very difficult times, and all the more credit to him that he has held out so long and done so much, not only as a manager but as a producer. He, like all mortals, has made his mistakes . . . but it would be very churlish indeed not to say, now that he retires (but for a while I hope), that he has deserved well of our modern drama, and that he has given greater opportunities to aspiring playwrights than—I will not say all, but a good bunch of the London theatres together. From the first, through no fault of his, Mr. MacDermott had to cumber himself with a laborious, I could almost say an impossible, machinery of administration. . . . It is a heavy task for a man to cope with these as well as selecting and producing plays. But it is not necessary to go into all the vicissitudes of Everyman. Some are known; some, no doubt, will come to light when Mr. MacDermott commits his experiences to book and history.

Illustrated London News, 16 January, 1926

Calendar of Plays

performed at the Everyman Theatre 1920–1926
under the management of Norman MacDermott

It can be assumed that performances were given Monday–Saturday evenings and Saturday matinées (public holidays excluded) between the dates shown, unless otherwise indicated.

The list excludes transfers by the company to other theatres in London and tours in Great Britain and on the continent. Where no production is listed the theatre was closed. 'Lets' or 'By Arrangement' productions are indicated *.

1920

15.9–18.9	*The Bonds of Interest*	Jacinto Benavente
20.9–22.9	*The Tragedy of Nan*	John Masefield
23.9–29.9	*You Never Can Tell*	Bernard Shaw
30.9–6.10	*Bonds of Interest*	Jacinto Benavente
7.10–9.10	*The Tragedy of Nan*	John Masefield
11.10–20.10	*You Never Can Tell*	Bernard Shaw
21.10–27.10	*Foundations* and *The Little Man*	John Galsworthy
28.10–30.10	*Bonds of Interest*	Jacinto Benavente
1.11–3.11	*The Tragedy of Nan*	John Masefield
4.11–10.11	*Foundations* and *The Little Man*	John Galsworthy
11.11–17.11	*You Never Can Tell*	Bernard Shaw
18.11–4.12	*Romeo and Juliet*	Shakespeare
6.12–18.12	*The Melting Pot*	Israel Zangwill
20.12–23.12	{ *The Honeymoon*	Arnold Bennett
	{ *Kind Heart and Coronet*	James Sterndale
24.12	*Nativity Play*	E. K. Chambers
27.12	*Through the Crack*	Algernon Blackwood and Violet Pearn
28.12–31.12	*Nativity Play*	E. K. Chambers
28.12–31.12 (matinées)	*Through the Crack*	Algernon Blackwood and Violet Pearn

1921

1.1–8.1 (twice daily)	*Through the Crack*	Algernon Blackwood and Violet Pearn
10.1–15.1 (matinées)	*Through the Crack*	Algernon Blackwood and Violet Pearn
10.1–22.1	*The Honeymoon*	Arnold Bennett
24.1–5.2	*You Never Can Tell*	Bernard Shaw
7.2–12.2	*Candida*	Bernard Shaw
14.2–19.2	*You Never Can Tell*	Bernard Shaw
21.2–5.3	*The Doctor's Dilemma*	Bernard Shaw
7.3–12.3	*Candida*	Bernard Shaw
14.3–2.4	*The Shewing-up of Blanco Posnet* *How he lied to her Husband* *The Dark Lady of the Sonnets*	Bernard Shaw
4.4–16.4	*The Doctor's Dilemma*	Bernard Shaw
18.4–30.4	*Major Barbara*	Bernard Shaw
23.4	Shakespeare Anniversary performances	
2.5–7.5	*The Toast* *Reggie Reforms*	Irene Bubna Irene Bubna and E. Camiller
9.5–21.5	*Major Barbara*	Bernard Shaw
23.5–14.6	*Man and Superman*	Bernard Shaw
15.6–2.7	*The Pedlar's Basket* including *Bushido* *A Farewell Supper* *In the Zone* *The Red Feather* *Jealous Barbouillé*	M. C. Marcus Arthur Schnitzler Eugene O'Neill A. A. Milne Molière
11.7–16.7	*A Doll's House*	Ibsen

The International Season:

4.10–29.10	*Diff'rent* *Suppressed Desires*	Eugene O'Neill Geo. Cram Cooke and Susan Glaspell
31.10–12.11	*The Race with the Shadow*	Wilhelm von Scholz
15.11–10.12	*Cheeso, The Tents of the Arabs, A Night at an Inn,* and *The Lost Silk Hat*	Lord Dunsany
6.12–10.12 (matinées)	*John Gabriel Borkman*	Ibsen
12.12–17.12	*John Gabriel Borkman*	Ibsen
26.12–31.12 (matinées) (evenings)	*The Shadow of the Glen* *The Building Fund* *Prunella*	J. M. Synge William Boyle Granville Barker and Laurence Housman

1922
The International Season—*contd.*

2.1–21.1	*The Shadow of the Glen*	J. M. Synge
(matinées)	*The Building Fund*	William Boyle
(evenings)	*Prunella* (cast change 9.1)	Granville Barker and
		Laurence Housman
23.1–4.2	*Mixed Marriage*	St. John Ervine
6.2–4.3	*Fanny's First Play*	Bernard Shaw
6.3–25.3	*Arms and the Man*	Bernard Shaw
27.3–17.4	*Getting Married*	Bernard Shaw
	Defeat	John Galsworthy
17.4–22.4	*Ile*	Eugene O'Neill
(matinées)	*The Bargain*	Walter Meade
	Daily Bread	Jules Renard, *trans.*
		Vaughan Thomas
18.4–10.5	*Misalliance*	Bernard Shaw
11.5–15.5	*The Pigeon*	John Galsworthy
16.5–20.5	*You Never Can Tell*	Bernard Shaw
22.5–3.6	*Hedda Gabler*	Ibsen
5.6–17.6	*You Never Can Tell*	Bernard Shaw
	Marlowe Dramatic Society in	
19.6–24.6	*Troilus and Cressida*	Shakespeare
	Daily Bread	Jules Renard, *trans.*
		Vaughan Thomas
17.7–22.7	*In the Zone*	Eugene O'Neill
	Suppressed Desires	Geo. Cram Cook and
		Susan Glaspell
24.7–5.8	*Candida*	Bernard Shaw
7.8–19.8	*The New Sin*	B. Macdonald Hastings
	The Constant Lover	St. John Irvine
21.8–2.9	*A Doll's House*	Ibsen
4.9–23.9	*Widowers' Houses*	Bernard Shaw
25.9–9.12	*Mary Stuart*	John Drinkwater
20.12–30.12	*Brer Rabbit*	Mabel Dearmer and
(matinées)		Martin Shaw
22.12–30.12	*Twelfth Night*	Shakespeare

1923

1.1–6.1	*Brer Rabbit*	Dearmer–Shaw
(matinées)		
(evenings)	*Twelfth Night*	Shakespeare
10.1–20.1	*Medium*	Leopold Thoma
	The Perfect Day	Emile Mazaud
29.1–17.2	*The Philanderer*	Bernard Shaw
19.2–10.3	*At Mrs. Beam's*	C. K. Munro
12.3–24.3	*The Alternative**	Lucy Wilson and
		Adrian Alington

1923—*contd.*

2.4–28.4	*The Doctor's Dilemma*	Bernard Shaw
30.4–26.5	*T'Marsdens*	James Gregson
28.5–16.6	*Major Barbara*	Bernard Shaw
	Private Performance:	
17.6	*Beyond Human Power*	Bjornsterne Bjornsen
18.6–7.7	*Candida*	Bernard Shaw
9.7–28.7	*Fanny's First Play*	Bernard Shaw
30.7–18.8	*Mary Stuart* (revival)	John Drinkwater
20.8–15.9	*Magic*	G. K. Chesterton
17.9–29.9	*Outward Bound*	Sutton Vane
1.10–17.10	*Ancient Lights**	Edward Percy
19.10–3.11	*What the Public Wants**	Arnold Bennett
8.11–17.11	*The Second Round*	Halcott Glover
29.11–12.12	*The Morals of Vanda**	May Hazel Marshall
18.12	*The Mask and the Face*	C. B. Fernald
	(Copyright Performance)	
21.12–31.12	*Love in a Village**	Isaac Bickerstaffe
		Dr. Arne, *arr.*
		Julian Herbage

1924

1.1–5.1	*Love in a Village**	Bickerstaffe–Arne,
		arr. Julian Herbage
12.1–19.1	*The Painted Lady**	Vera Beringer
5.2–15.3	*The Mask and the Face*	C. B. Fernald
17.3–29.3	*Young Imeson**	J. R. Gregson
4.4–7.4	*Monica**	Ernest Cecil
16.4–17.5	*In and Out**	Brandon Fleming
23.5–4.6	*The Tropic Line**	Noel Shammon
11.6–21.6	*The Man of Destiny* and *Augustus does his bit*	} Bernard Shaw
24.6–5.7	*Her Daughter**	John Peterson
8.7	*Arms and the Man*	Bernard Shaw
	(Charity Performance)	
9.7–9.8	*Getting Married*	Bernard Shaw
12.8–16.8	*Low Tide*	Ernest George
27.8–30.8	*The Man of Destiny* and *How he lied to her Husband*	} Bernard Shaw
11.9–20.9	*False Values**	Lechmere Worral
24.9–18.10	*The Devil's Disciple*	Bernard Shaw
27.10–8.11	*Misalliance*	Bernard Shaw
10.11–22.11	*Clogs to Clogs**	John Walton
25.11–13.12	*The Vortex*	Noel Coward
16.12–22.12	*The Tyranny of Home**	W. Lemon Hall
26.12–31.12	*The Philanderer*	Bernard Shaw

1925

1.1–10.1	*The Philanderer*	Bernard Shaw
20.1–7.2	"*Home Affairs*"	Ladislas Fodor, *trans.* Norman MacDermott
10.2–19.2	*Yvelle**	Margaret Clement Scott and C. B. Fernald
24.2–7.3	*It happened in Ardoran**	Ann Stephenson and Allan Macbeth
16.3–4.4	*The Painted Swan*	Elizabeth Bibesco
11.4–25.4	*Overture**	Sutton Vane
6.5–9.5	*The Swallow*	Viola Tree
16.5–6.6	*Magic*	G. K. Chesterton
12.6–20.6	*Diff'rent* and *The Long Voyage Home*	} Eugene O'Neill

The Sybil Arundale Season:

30.6–14.7	*The Wild Duck**	Ibsen
15.7–1.8	*Henry IV**	Luigi Pirandello
3.8–15.8	*Caste**	T. W. Robertson
17.8–22.8	*Mirandolina**	Goldoni, *adapted* by Lady Gregory
28.8–12.9	*I'll tell the World**	Reginald Purdell and Edwin Henderson
14.9–19.9	*The Sybarite**	F. Kinsey Peile
22.9–3.10	*The Limpet**	Vernon Woodhouse and Victor MacClure

13.10–31.10	*Ghosts*	Ibsen
3.11–14.11	*The Dark Angel*	Guy Bolton
1.12–5.12	*Sweet Pepper*	Geoffrey Moss
14.12–19.12	*Sweet Pepper* (New Production)	Geoffrey Moss
28.12–31.12	The Liverpool Repertory Theatre Company in *Inheritors*	Susan Glaspell

1926

1.1–16.1	*Inheritors*	Susan Glaspell
20.1–30.1	*The Man who was Thursday*	Mrs. Cecil Chesterton and Ralph Neale

Actors and Actresses

A roll of artistes who appeared at the Everyman Theatre
during the period 1920–1926

This list has been compiled by direct transcription from the cast lists
in programmes. The ubiquitous Walter Plinge makes his appearance to
serve as a warning that there may be other unidentified colleagues of
his among the lesser-known names.

Peggy Abbot, J. R. Ackerley, Angus Adams, Miriam Adams, Frank
Ainslie, Muriel Alexander, Muriel Allen, Sarah Allgood, Claud
Allister, Herbert Anstey, Harold Anstruther, Stella Arbenina,
Elizabeth Arkell, William Armstrong, Emmie Arthur-Williams,
Grace Arundale, Sybil Arundale, D. D. Arundell, Frank Atherley,
Felix Aylmer, Louise Ayrton, Randle Ayrton

Reginald Bach, Angela Baddeley, Gordon Bailey, Julian Bainbridge,
Leslie J. Banks, Miss Banks, C. J. Barber, Ivor Barnard, Orlando
Barnett, J. J. Bartlett, Dora Barton, Mary Barton, Leah Bateman,
Hilda Bayley, Claud Beerbohm, T. B. Belk, Ivy Bell, Charles Bennett,
Esme Beringer, A. Bettini, Geoffrey Bevan, D. H. Beves, Vera Birch,
Richard Bird, Seton Blackden, John C. Bland, Sydney Bland, Ruth
Bower, Helen Boyce, William Bradford, Lilian Braithwaite, Amy
Brandon-Thomas, Vincent Breit, Edmond Breon, Honor Bright,
Harry Bristow, Hutin Britton, Neville Brook, E. H. Brooke, Albert
Brouett, David Brynley, Ronald Buchanan, Babs Buddon, Douglas
Burbidge, G. F. Burgess, Ann Butler, Walter Butler, Roy Byford,
A. L. Byrne, Cecily Byrne

Jean Cadell, Audrey Cameron, Cecil Cameron, Iné Cameron, Mrs.
Patrick Campbell, Clive Carey, George G. Carr, J. Murray Carrington,
Leo G. Carroll, Charles Carson, Audrey Carten, Margaret Carter,
Nell Carter, Peggy Carter, Jeanne de Casalis, Owen Cassidy, Billy
Casson, Chris Castor, Frank Cellier, Irene Chandley, Dorothy Cheston,
Frances Clare, O. B. Clarence, Alfred Clark, Hannam Clark, Percival
Clarke, Frank Clewlow, V. C. Clinton Baddeley, Vera Clinton
Baddeley, Hayden Coffin, Richard Coke, Ethel Coleridge, Raymonde
Collignon, Madge Compton, Edward Cooper, Frederick T. Cooper,
Guy Cooper, Janet Cooper, Daisy Cordell, Noël Coward, Laura
Cowie, Robert Craig, Lilian Cramphorn, Oliver Crombie, Evelyn
Culver, Basil Cunard, Cyril Cunningham

Marie Dainton, Noel Dainton, Margaret Damer, Reginald Dance, Dirk Daniell, Granville Darling, Irene Darrell, Bromley Davenport, Gilbert Davis, Doris Dean, Margaret Dean, Violet Dean, Reginald Denham, J. E. T. Denman, Clifford Desboro, Philip Desborough, Ernest P. Digges, Daniel Dirk, Miss Disney, D. H. Dixon, Joseph A. Dodd, A. Doddington, Edmée Dormeuil, Henry Downes, Fabia Drake, Stanley Drewitt, Greta Drudge, Lola Duncan, Geoffrey Dunlop, Franklin Dyall

George Elton, Daisy England, Edith Evans, Eileen Everson, Stephen T. Ewart

Faith Faber, Joyce Fagan, Sydney Fairbrother, Lettice Fairfax, Violet Farebrother, Helen Ferres, Gladys Ffolliett, Alexander Field, Beatrix Filmer, Thurlow Finn, J. Fisher-White, Gilly Flower, Laurence Foley, Mary Forbes, Jean Forbes-Robertson, Matthew Forsyth, Greta Foster, Huz Foster-Cameron, Cecil Fowler, Judith Fowler, Frank Freeman, J. Leslie Frith

Marjorie Gabain, H. R. Gardiner, Reginald Gardiner, John Garside, Robert Glennie, Neta Glynne, Peter Godfrey, A. Goodden, P. Goodyer, Marjorie Gordon, Theresa Gorringe, John Goss, Violet Gould, Claude Graham, Roy Graham, Violet Graham, Ailsa Grahame, Roland Grant, Alfred Gray, Dorothy Green, Clare Greet, James R. Gregson, W. Earle Grey, Cyril Grier, Ethel Griffies, Charles Groves, Campbell Gullan

Ernest Haines, Ernest Hamit, Diana Hamilton, Harry Hampson, Louise Hampton, Nicholas Hannen, Laurence Hanray, Gordon Harker, Edith Harley, E. Harman, Alfred Harris, Clare Harris, Robert Harris, Patrick Harvey, Louis Harvey-James, George Hayes, Lois Heatherley, Clifford Heatherley, Julian Herbage, Walter Herbage, Patrick Herbert, Grizelda Hervey, Tom Heslewood, Muriel Hewitt, H. R. Hignett, Gwendolin Hill, Carleton Hobbs, Phoebe Hodgson, Michael Hogan, Louise Holbrook, Alan Hollis, Anthony Hollis, Baliol Holloway, Dorothy Holmes-Gore, A. S. Homewood, Dorothy Hope, Dennis Hosking, George Howard, Esme Hubbard, Walter Hudd, Mary Hughes, D. S. Hunt, P. Hunter

Jean Imray, Winifred Izard

Sylvia Jackson, Miss Jacobs, Isabel Jeans, Alan Jeayes, Douglas Jefferies, Jeff Jeffries, Aida Jenoure, Gerald Jerome, Mervyn Johns, G. Johnston-Campbell, Maude Jolliffe, Hazel Jones

Arthur Karnon, Claire Keep, Mary Kellas, Henry Kendall, William Kendall, Agatha Kentish, Nancy Kenyon, Neil Kenyon, Molly Kerr, William Kershaw, Gertrude Kingston, Charles Koop

C. Landeau, Elissa Landi, Herman de Lange, Leila Langley, Stanley Lathbury, Paige Lawrence, C. E. A. Lea, Auriol Lee, Rupert Lee, Guy le Feuvre, Frederick Leister, Irene Lemon, Cressie Leonard, J. Hubert Leslie, Victor H. Leslie, Edith Lester-Jones, F. Lewis, Eileen Lighthorne, Mona Limerick, Roger Livesey, Fewlass Llewellyn, Doris Lloyd, Basil Loder, Basil Lofting, Herbert Lomas, Eric Lugg, Joan Luxton, Parker K. Lynch, Betty Lynn

Allan Macbeth, Moyna Macgill, Gordon Macleod, Randolph Maherd, Ernest Mainwaring, Lauderdale Maitland, Eliot Makeham, Nadine March, G. D. St. Q. Marescaux, Charles Marford, Celia Marlow, Nan Marriott-Watson, Herbert Marshall, T. H. Marshall, Dorothy Martin, A. E. Maschwitz, Raymond Massey, Dorothy Massingham, Aubrey Mather, Betty Maude, Hilda Maude, Adela Mavis, Renée Mayer, Harold B. Meade, Walter Meade, Dodd Mehan, Mary Merrall, George Merritt, Randolph McLeod, Adelqui Miller, Elizabeth Milner, Ernest Milton, Margaret Moffat, Clifford Mollison, William Mollison, William Monk, Frank Moore, Hilda Moore, Primrose Morgan, Noel Morris, Phyllis Morris, Charles Mortimer, Edwin Morton, Basil Moss, Frederick Moyes, G. H. Mulcaster

Cyril Nash, Cathleen Nesbitt, H. St. D. Nettleton, J. Cranstoun Neville, H. O. Nicholson, Nora Nicholson, Ronald Nicholson, Matthew Norgate, Grosvenor North

Cicely Oates, Terence O'Brien, Una O'Conner, Desmond O'Donovan, Fred O'Donovan, Ellen O'Malley, Henry Oscar

Arthur Page, Cecil Parker, Dorothy Passmore, Rosalind Patrick, Joyce Pearce, J. Kinsey Peile, Constance Pelissier, Gerald Pemberton, R. A. Penrose, Joan Pereira, Dorothy Peters, Edward Petley, Frank Petley, Frank Pettingell, Francis Phair, Marian Phillips, E. Philpot, [Walter Plinge], Elizabeth Pollock, Ellen Pollock, Muriel Pope, Ruth Povah, Bryan Powley, Muriel Pratt, Nancy Price, William Pringle, C. Vernon Proctor, Arthur Pusey

Charles Quartermaine

Henzie Raeburn, Michael Raghan, James Raglan, Jack Raine, Claude Rains, Mlle. [Marie] Rambert, Muriel Randall, Boris Ranevsky, Tristan Rawson, Percy Rhodes, Roy Rich, Charles Rider, Edward Rigby, Reginald Rivington, Evelyn Roberts, J. H. Roberts, D. H. Robertson, Norah Robinson, Mary Robson, Marcelle Roche, Dan F. Roe, Irene Rooke, Evelyn Roselle, Milton Rosmer, Mrs. Ross-Campbell Frank Royde, Dorothy Rundell, M. A. Rushton, Lilian Russel, Dora Russell, G. H. W. Rylands

Dorothy Sainsbury, Ivan Samson, Ewert Scott, Harold Scott, A. Scott-Gatty, Wilfred Seagram, Russell Sedgwick, Morton Selten, Dorothea Seton, Athene Seyler, F. B. J. Sharp, Innis Shawen, Leonard Shepherd, Michael Sherbrooke, Jeanette Sherwin, Margot Sieveking, Millie Sim, Ronald Simpson, Sinna Sinclair, Olga Slade, Olive Sloane, Beatrice Smith, Dodie Smith, Nance Smyth-Greenwood, Madge Snell, T. W. Southam, Helen Spencer, William Stack, Charles A. Staite, S. Victor Stanley, Marjorie Stanley-Clarke, Ann Stephenson, Athole Stewart, W. Edward Stirling, H. G. Stoker, Phyllis Stuckey, Margaret Swallow, Mercia Swinburne, Ion Swinley

Barbara Tallermon, Victor Tandy, Mrs. A. B. Tapping, Lillian Taylor, Joyce Templeton, Ellen Terry, Mabel Terry-Lewis, Ernest Thesiger, Agnes Thomas, Charles Thomas, Alec F. Thompson, Beatrix Thomson Gwen Tremayne, Ann Trevor, John R. Turnbull, Lilian Tweed, Cyril Twyford

Mimosa Valentine, Sutton Vane, Una Venning, Arthur Vezin, Joan Vivian Rees, Frank Vosper

Philip Wade, Laura Walker, Muriel Walker, George Waller, Herbert Waring, Dorothy Warren, Lady Maud Warrender, Margaret Watson, Ben Webster, Peggy Webster, Algernon West, Frances Wetherall, Vivienne Whitaker, [Dame] May Whitty, Andrew Wight, Elizabeth Williams, Harcourt Williams, Hugh Williams. John Williams, Brember Wills, Josephine Wilson, J. B. Wilson, Lucy Wilson, Geoffrey Wincott, Godfrey Winn, Jane Wood, Dorothy Wordsworth, George S. Wray, Andrew Wright, Hugh E. Wright, Arthur Wynn, Aileen Wyse

Margaret Yarde

Index

The Index omits all references to the Everyman Theatre and to the author, Norman MacDermott. Except for those mentioned in the narrative of the book, it also excludes the titles of plays, and names of actors and actresses, contained in the sample Casts and Reviews, the Calendar and alphabetical list printed on pages 112–132.